The Epistles of St. Ignatius

The Epistles of St. Ignatius

St. Ignatius

The Epistles of St. Ignatius

© Lighthouse Publishing 2019

Written by: St. Ignatius (A.D. 30 – 107)
Edited by: Alexander Roberts, D.D. (May 12th, 1826 – March 8th, 1901)
Edited by: James Donaldson, LL.D. (April 26th, 1831 – March 1915)
Updated into Modern U.S English: A.M. Overett (b. 1960)

All rights reserved. Without limiting the rights under copyright reserved above, no part of this publication may be reproduced, stored in a retrieval system, or transmitted, in any form or by any means (electronic, mechanical, photocopying, recording or otherwise), without the prior written permission of the copyright owner of this book.

Published by
Lighthouse Publishing
SAN 257-4330
5531 Dufferin Drive
Savage, Minnesota, 55378
United States of America

www.lighthouseebooks.com

Introductory Note to the Epistles of Ignatius

[A.d.30–107.] The seductive myth which represents this Father as the little child whom the Lord placed in the midst of his apostles (St. Matt. xviii. 2) indicates at least the period when he may be supposed to have been born. That he and Polycarp were fellow-disciples under St. John, is a tradition by no means inconsistent with anything in the Epistles of either. His subsequent history is sufficiently indicated in the Epistles which follow. Had not the plan of this series been so exclusively that of a mere revised reprint, the writings of Ignatius themselves would have made me diffident as to the undertaking. It seems impossible for anyone to write upon the subject of these precious remains, without provoking controversy. This publication is designed as an Eirenicon, and hence "few words are best," from one who might be supposed incapable of an unbiased opinion on most of the points which have been raised in connection with these Epistles. I must content myself therefore, by referring the studious reader to the originals as edited by Bishop Jacobson, with a Latin version and copious annotations. That revered and learned divine honored me with his friendship; and his precious edition has been my frequent study, with theological students, almost ever since it appeared in 1840. It is by no means superannuated by the vigorous Ignatian literature which has since sprung up, and to which reference will he made elsewhere. But I am content to leave the whole matter, without comment, to the minds of Christians of whatever school and to their independent conclusions. It is a great thing to present them in a single volume with the shorter and longer Epistles duly compared, and with the Curetonian version besides. One luxury only I may claim, to relieve the drudging task-work of a mere reviser. Surely I may point out some of the proverbial wisdom of this great disciple, which has often stirred my soul, as with the trumpet heard by St. John in Patmos. In him, indeed, the lions encountered a lion, one truly begotten of "the Lion of the tribe of Judah." Take, then, as a specimen, these thrilling injunctions from his letter to Polycarp, to whom he bequeathed his own spirit, and in whom he well knew the Church would recognize a sort of survival of St. John himself. If the reader has any true perception of the rhythm and force of the Greek language, let him learn by heart the originals of the following aphorisms:—

1 Find time to pray without ceasing.
2 Every wound is not healed with the same remedy.
3 The times demand thee, as pilots the haven.
4 The crown is immortality.
5 Stand like a beaten anvil.
6 It is the part of a good athlete to be bruised and to prevail.
7 Consider the times: look for Him who is above time.
8 Slight not the menservants and the handmaids.
9 Let your stewardship define your work.
10 A Christian is not his own master, but waits upon God.

Ignatius so delighted in his name Theophorus (sufficiently expounded in his own words to Trajan or his official representative), that it is worth noting how deeply the early Christians felt and believed in (2 Cor. vi. 16) the indwelling Spirit.

Ignatius has been censured for his language to the

Romans, in which he seems to crave martyrdom. But he was already condemned, in law a dead man, and felt himself at liberty to glory in his tribulations. Is it more than modern Christians often too lightly sing? —

"Let cares like a wild deluge come,
And storms of sorrow fall," etc.

So the holy martyr adds, "Only let me attain unto Jesus Christ."

The Epistle to the Romans is utterly inconsistent with any conception on his part, that Rome was the see and residence of a bishop holding any other than fraternal relations with himself. It is very noteworthy that it is devoid of expressions, elsewhere made emphatic, which would have been much insisted upon had they been found herein. Think what use would have been made of it, had the words which he addresses to the Smyrnæans (chap. viii.) to strengthen their fidelity to Polycarp, been found in this letter to the Romans, especially as in this letter we first find the use of the phrase "Catholic Church" in patristic writings. He defines it as to be found "where Jesus Christ is," words which certainly do not limit it to communion with a professed successor of St. Peter.

The following is the original Introductory Notice:—

The epistles ascribed to Ignatius have given rise to more controversy than any other documents connected with the primitive Church. As is evident to every reader on the very first glance at these writings, they contain numerous statements which bear on points of ecclesiastical order that have long divided the Christian world; and a strong temptation has thus been felt to allow some amount of prepossession to enter into the discussion of their authenticity or spuriousness. At the same time, this question has furnished a noble field for the display of learning and acuteness, and has, in the various forms under which it has been debated, given rise to not a few works of the very highest ability and scholarship. We shall present such an outline of the controversy as may enable the reader to understand its position at the present day.

There are, in all, fifteen Epistles which bear the name of Ignatius. These are the following: One to the Virgin Mary, two to the Apostle John, one to Mary of Cassobelæ, one to the Tarsians, one to the Antiochians, one to Hero, a deacon of Antioch, one to the Philippians; one to the Ephesians, one to the Magnesians, one to the Trallians, one to the Romans, one to the Philadelphians, one to the Smyrnæans, and one to Polycarp. The first three exist only in Latin: all the rest are extant also in Greek.

It is now the universal opinion of critics, that the first eight of these professedly Ignatian letters are spurious. They bear in themselves indubitable proofs of being the production of a later age than that in which Ignatius lived. Neither Eusebius nor Jerome makes the least reference to them; and they are now by common consent set aside as forgeries, which were at various dates, and to serve special purposes, put forth under the name of the celebrated Bishop of Antioch.

But after the question has been thus simplified, it still remains sufficiently complex. Of the seven Epistles which are acknowledged by Eusebius (Hist. Eccl., iii. 36), we possess two Greek recensions, a shorter and a longer. It is plain that one or other of these exhibits a corrupt text, and scholars have for the most part agreed to accept the shorter form as representing the genuine letters of Ignatius. This was the opinion generally acquiesced in, from the time when critical editions of these Epistles began to be issued, down to our own day. Criticism, indeed, fluctuated a good deal as to which Epistles should be accepted and which rejected. Archp. Usher (1644), Isaac Vossius (1646), J. B. Cotelerius (1672), Dr. T. Smith (1709), and others, edited the writings ascribed to Ignatius in forms differing very considerably as to the order in which they were arranged, and the degree of authority assigned them, until at length, from about the beginning of the eighteenth century, the seven Greek Epistles, of which a translation is here given, came to be generally accepted in their shorter form as the genuine writings of Ignatius.

Before this date, however, there had not been wanting some who refused to acknowledge the authenticity of these Epistles in either of the recensions in which they were then known to exist. By far the most learned and elaborate work maintaining this position was that of Daillé (or Dallæus), published in 1666. This drew forth in reply the celebrated Vindiciæ of Bishop Pearson, which appeared in 1672. It was generally supposed that this latter work had established on an immoveable foundation the genuineness of the shorter form of the Ignatian Epistles; and, as we have stated above, this was the conclusion almost universally accepted down to our own day. The only considerable exception to this concurrence was presented by Whiston, who labored to maintain in his Primitive Christianity Revived (1711) the superior claims of the longer recension of the Epistles, apparently influenced in doing so by the support which he thought they furnished to the kind of Arianism which he had adopted.

But although the shorter form of the Ignatian letters had been generally accepted in preference to the longer, there was still a pretty prevalent opinion among scholars, that even it could not be regarded as absolutely free from interpolations, or as of undoubted authenticity. Thus said Lardner, in his Credibility of the Gospel History (1743): "have carefully compared the two editions, and am very well satisfied, upon that comparison, that the larger are an interpolation of the smaller, and not the smaller an epitome or abridgment of the larger. ... But whether the smaller themselves are the genuine writings of Ignatius, Bishop of Antioch, is a question that has been much disputed, and has employed the pens of the ablest critics. And whatever positiveness some may have shown on either side, I must own I have found it a very difficult question."

This expression of uncertainty was repeated in substance by Jortin (1751), Mosheim (1755), Griesbach (1768), Rosenmüller (1795), Neander (1826), and many others; some going so far as to deny that we have any authentic remains of Ignatius at all, while others, though admitting the seven shorter letters as being probably his, yet strongly suspected that they were not free from interpolation. Upon the whole, however, the shorter recension was, until recently, accepted without much opposition, and chiefly in dependence on the work of Bishop Pearson above mentioned, as exhibiting the genuine form of the Epistles of Ignatius. But a totally different aspect was given to the question by the discovery of a Syriac version of three of these Epistles among the Mss. Procured from the monastery of St. Mary

St. Ignatius

Deipara, in the desert of Nitria, in Egypt. In the years 1838, 1839, and again in 1842, Archdeacon Tattam visited that monastery, and succeeded in obtaining for the English Government a vast number of ancient Syriac manuscripts. On these being deposited in the British Museum, the late Dr. Cureton, who then had charge of the Syriac department, discovered among them, first, the Epistle to Polycarp, and then again, the same Epistle, with those to the Ephesians and to the Romans, in two other volumes of manuscripts.

As the result of this discovery, Cureton published in 1845 a work, entitled, The Ancient Syriac Version of the Epistles of St. Ignatius to Polycarp, the Ephesian, and the Romans, etc., in which he argued that these Epistles represented more accurately than any formerly published what Ignatius had actually written. This, of course, opened up the controversy afresh. While some accepted the views of Cureton, others very strenuously opposed them. Among the former was the late Chev. Bunsen; among the latter, an anonymous writer in the English Review, and Dr. Hefele, in his third edition of the Apostolic Fathers. In reply to those who had controverted his arguments, Cureton published his Vindiciæ Ignatianæ in 1846, and his Corpus Ignatianumin 1849. He begins his introduction to the last-named work with the following sentences: "Exactly three centuries and a half intervened between the time when three Epistles in Latin, attributed to St. Ignatius, first issued from the press, and the publication in 1845 of three letters in Syriac bearing the name of the same apostolic writer. Very few years passed before the former were almost universally regarded as false and spurious; and it seems not improbable that scarcely a longer period will elapse before the latter be

7

almost as generally acknowledged and received as the only true and genuine letters of the venerable Bishop of Antioch that have either come down to our times, or were ever known in the earliest ages of the Christian Church."

Had the somewhat sanguine hope thus expressed been realized, it would have been unnecessary for us to present to the English reader more than a translation of these three Syriac Epistles. But the Ignatian controversy is not yet settled. There are still those who hold that the balance of argument is in favor of the shorter Greek, as against these Syriac Epistles. They regard the latter as an epitome of the former, and think the harshness which, according to them, exists in the sequence of thoughts and sentences, clearly shows that this is the case. We have therefore given all the forms of the Ignatian letters which have the least claim on our attention. The reader may judge, by comparison for himself, which of these is to be accepted as genuine, supposing him disposed to admit the claims of any one of them. We content ourselves with laying the materials for judgment before him, and with referring to the above-named works in which we find the whole subject discussed. As to the personal history of Ignatius, almost nothing is known. The principal source of information regarding him is found in the account of his martyrdom, to which the reader is referred. Polycarp alludes to him in his Epistle to the Philippians (chap. ix.), and also to his letters (chap. xiii.). Irenæus quotes a passage from his Epistle to the Romans (Adv. Hær., v. 28; Epist. ad Rom., chap. iv.), without, however, naming him. Origen twice refers to him, first in the preface to his Comm. on the Song of Solomon, where he quotes a passage from the Epistle of Ignatius to the Romans, and again in his sixth homily on St. Luke, where he quotes from the Epistle to the Ephesians, both times naming the author. It is unnecessary to give later references. Supposing the letters of Ignatius and the account of his martyrdom to be authentic, we learn from them that he voluntarily presented himself before Trajan at Antioch, the seat of his bishopric, when that prince was on his first expedition against the Parthians and Armenians (a.d. 107); and on professing himself a Christian, was condemned to the wild beasts. After a long and dangerous voyage he came to Smyrna, of which Polycarp was bishop, and thence wrote his four Epistles to the Ephesians, the Magnesians, the Trallians, and the Romans. From Smyrna he came to Troas, and tarrying there a few days, he wrote to the Philadelphians, the Smyrnæans, and Polycarp. He then came on to Neapolis, and passed through the whole of Macedonia. Finding a ship at Dyrrachium in Epirus about to sail into Italy, he embarked, and crossing the Adriatic, was brought to Rome, where he perished on the 20th of December 107, or, as some think, who deny a twofold expedition of Trajan against the Parthians, on the same day of the year a.d.116.

The Epistle of Ignatius to the Ephesians Shorter and Longer Versions

Ignatius, who is also called Theophorus, to the Church which is at Ephesus, in Asia, deservedly most happy, being blessed in the greatness and fullness of God the Father, and predestinated before the beginning of time, that it should be always for an enduring and unchangeable glory, being united and elected through the true passion by the will of the Father, and Jesus Christ, our God: Abundant happiness through Jesus Christ, and His undefiled grace.

Ignatius, who is also called Theophorus, to the Church which is at Ephesus, in Asia, deservedly most happy, being blessed in the greatness and fullness of God the Father, and predestinated before the beginning of time, that it should be always for an enduring and unchangeable glory, being united and elected through the true passion by the will of God the Father, and of our Lord Jesus Christ our Savior: Abundant happiness through Jesus Christ, and His undefiled joy.

Chapter I.—Praise of the Ephesians.

I have become acquainted with your name, much-beloved in God, which ye have acquired by the habit of righteousness, according to the faith and love in Jesus Christ our Savior. Being the followers of God, and stirring up yourselves by the blood of God, ye have perfectly accomplished the work which was beseeming to you. For, on hearing that I came bound from Syria for the common name and hope, trusting through your prayers to be permitted to fight with beasts at Rome, that so by martyrdom I may indeed become the disciple of Him "who gave Himself for us, an offering and sacrifice to God," [ye hastened to see me]. I received, therefore, your whole multitude in the name of God, through Onesimus, a man of inexpressible love, and your bishop in the flesh, whom I pray you by Jesus Christ to love, and that you would all seek to be like him. And blessed be He who has granted unto you, being worthy, to obtain such an excellent bishop.

I have become acquainted with your greatly-desired name in God, which ye have acquired by the habit of righteousness, according to the faith and love in Christ Jesus our Savior. Being the followers of the love of God towards man, and stirring up yourselves by the blood of Christ, you have perfectly accomplished the work which was beseeming to you. For, on hearing that I came bound from Syria for the sake of Christ, our common hope, trusting through your prayers to be permitted to fight with beasts at Rome, that so by martyrdom I may indeed become the disciple of Him "who gave Himself for us, an offering and a sacrifice to God," [ye hastened to see me]. I have therefore received your whole multitude in the name of God, through Onesimus, a man of inexpressible love, and who is your bishop, whom I pray you by Jesus Christ to love, and that you would all seek to be like him. Blessed be God, who has granted unto you, who are yourselves so excellent, to obtain such an excellent bishop.

Chapter II.—Congratulations and entreaties.

As to my fellow-servant Burrhus, your deacon in regard to God and blessed in all things, I beg that he may continue longer, both for your honor and that of your bishop. And Crocus also, worthy both of God and you, whom I have received as the manifestation of your love, hath in all things refreshed me, as the Father of our Lord Jesus Christ shall also refresh him; together with Onesimus, and Burrhus, and Euplus, and Fronto, by means of whom, I have, as to love, beheld all of you. May I always have joy of you, if indeed I be worthy of it. It is therefore befitting that you should in every way glorify Jesus Christ, who hath glorified you, that by a unanimous obedience "ye may be perfectly joined together in the same mind, and in the same judgment, and may all speak the same thing concerning the same thing," and that, being subject to the bishop and the presbytery, ye may in all respects be sanctified.

As to our fellow-servant Burrhus, your deacon in regard to God and blessed in all things, I pray that he may continue blameless for the honor of the Church, and of your most blessed bishop. Crocus also, worthy both of God and you, whom we have received as the manifestation of your love to us, hath in all things refreshed me, and "hath not been ashamed of my chain," as the Father of our Lord Jesus Christ will also refresh him; together with Onesimus, and Burrhus, and Euplus, and Fronto, by means of whom I have, as to love, beheld all of you. May I always have joy of you, if indeed I be worthy of it. It is therefore befitting that you should in every way glorify Jesus Christ, who hath glorified you, that by a unanimous obedience "ye may be perfectly joined together in the same mind and in the same judgment, and may all speak the same thing concerning the same thing," and that, being subject to the bishop and the presbytery, ye may in all respects be sanctified.

Chapter III.—Exhortations to unity.

I do not issue orders to you, as if I were some great person. For though I am bound for the name [of Christ], I am not yet perfect in Jesus Christ. For now I begin to be a disciple, and I speak to you as fellow-disciples with me. For it was needful for me to have been stirred up by you in faith, exhortation, patience, and long-suffering. But inasmuch as love suffers me not to be silent in regard to you, I have therefore taken upon me first to exhort you that ye would all run together in accordance with the will of God. For even Jesus Christ, our inseparable life, is the [manifested] will of the Father; as also bishops, settled everywhere to the utmost bounds [of the earth], are so by the will of Jesus Christ.

I do not issue orders to you, as if I were some great person. For though I am bound for His name, I am not yet perfect in Jesus Christ. For now I begin to be a disciple, and I speak to you as my fellow-servants. For it was needful for me to have been admonished by you in faith, exhortation, patience, and long-suffering. But inasmuch as love suffers me not to be silent in regard to you, I have therefore taken upon me first to exhort you that ye would run together in accordance with the will of God. For even Jesus Christ does all things according to the will of the Father, as He Himself declares in a certain place, "I do always those things that please Him." Wherefore it behooves us also to live according to the will of God in Christ, and to imitate Him as Paul did. For, says he, "Be ye followers of me, even as I also am of Christ."

Chapter IV.—The same continued.

Wherefore it is fitting that ye should run together in accordance with the will of your bishop, which thing also ye do. For your justly renowned presbytery, worthy of God, is fitted as exactly to the bishop as the strings are to the harp. Therefore in your concord and harmonious love, Jesus Christ is sung. And do ye, man by man, become a choir, that being harmonious in love, and taking up the song of God in unison, ye may with one voice sing to the Father through Jesus Christ, so that He may both hear you, and perceive by your works that ye are indeed the members of His Son. It is profitable, therefore, that you should live in an unblameable unity, that thus ye may always enjoy communion with God.

Wherefore it is fitting that ye also should run together in accordance with the will of the bishop who by God's appointment rules over you. Which thing ye indeed of yourselves do, being instructed by the Spirit. For your justly-renowned presbytery, being worthy of God, is fitted as exactly to the bishop as the strings are to the harp. Thus, being joined together in concord and harmonious love, of which Jesus Christ is the Captain and Guardian, do ye, man by man, become but one choir; so that, agreeing together in concord, and obtaining a perfect unity with God, ye may indeed be one in harmonious feeling with God the Father, and His beloved Son Jesus Christ our Lord. For, says He, "Grant unto them, Holy Father, that as I and Thou are one, they also may be one in us." It is therefore profitable that you, being joined together with God in an unblameable unity, should be the followers of the example of Christ, of whom also ye are members.

Chapter V.—The praise of unity.

For if I in this brief space of time, have enjoyed such fellowship with your bishop —I mean not of a mere human, but of a spiritual nature—how much more do I reckon you happy who are so joined to him as the Church is to Jesus Christ, and as Jesus Christ is to the Father, that so all things may agree in unity! Let no man deceive himself: if anyone be not within the altar, he is deprived of the bread of God. For if the prayer of one or two possesses such power, how much more that of the bishop and the whole Church! He, therefore, that does not assemble with the Church, has even by this manifested his pride, and condemned himself. For it is written, "God resisted the proud." Let us be careful, then, not to set ourselves in opposition to the bishop, in order that we may be subject to God.

For if I, in this brief space of time, have enjoyed such fellowship with your bishop —I mean not of a mere human, but of a spiritual nature—how much more do I reckon you happy, who so depend on him as the Church does on the Lord Jesus, and the Lord does on God and His Father, that so all things may agree in unity! Let no man deceive himself: if anyone be not within the altar, he is deprived of the bread of God. For if the prayer of one or two possesses such power that Christ stands in the midst of them, how much more will the prayer of the bishop and of the whole Church, ascending up in harmony to God, prevail for the granting of all their petitions in Christ! He, therefore, that separates himself from such, and does not meet in the society where sacrifices are offered, and with "the Church of the first-born whose names are written in heaven," is a wolf in sheep's clothing, while he presents a mild outward appearance. Do ye, beloved, be careful to be subject to the bishop, and the presbyters and the deacons. For he that is subject to these is obedient to Christ, who has appointed them; but he that is disobedient to these is disobedient to Christ Jesus. And "he that obeyed not the Son shall not see life, but the wrath of God abided on him." For he that yields not obedience to his superiors is self-confident, quarrelsome, and proud. But "God," says [the Scripture] "resisted the proud, but giveth grace to the humble;" and, "The proud have greatly transgressed." The

Lord also says to the priests, "He that heareth you, heareth Me; and he that heareth Me, heareth the Father that sent Me. He that despises you, despises Me; and he that despises Me, despises Him that sent Me."

Chapter VI.—Have respect to the bishop as to Christ Himself.

Now the more anyone sees the bishop keeping silence, the more ought he to revere him. For we ought to receive everyone whom the Master of the house sends to be over His household, as we would do Him that sent him. It is manifest, therefore, that we should look upon the bishop even as we would upon the Lord Himself. And indeed Onesimus himself greatly commends your good order in God, that ye all live according to the truth, and that no sect has any dwelling-place among you. Nor, indeed, do ye hearken to anyone rather than to Jesus Christ speaking in truth. The more, therefore, you see the bishop silent, the more do you reverence him. For we ought to receive everyone whom the Master of the house sends to be over His household, as we would do Him that sent him. It is manifest, therefore, that we should look upon the bishop even as we would look upon the Lord Himself, standing, as he does, before the Lord. For "it behooves the man who looks carefully about him, and is active in his business, to stand before kings, and not to stand before slothful men." And indeed Onesimus himself greatly commends your good order in God, that ye all live according to the truth, and that no sect has any dwelling-place among you. Nor indeed do ye hearken to anyone rather than to Jesus Christ, the true Shepherd and Teacher. And ye are, as Paul wrote to you, "one body and one spirit, because ye have also been called in one hope of the faith. Since also "there is one Lord, one faith, one baptism, one God and Father of all, who is over all, and through all, and in all." Such, then, are ye, having been taught by such instructors, Paul the Christ bearer, and Timothy the most faithful.

Chapter VII.—Beware of false teachers.

For some are in the habit of carrying about the name [of Jesus Christ] in wicked guile, while yet they practice things unworthy of God, whom ye must flee as ye would wild beasts. For they are ravening dogs, who bite secretly, against whom ye must be on your guard, inasmuch as they are men who can scarcely be cured. There is one Physician who is possessed both of flesh and spirit; both made and not made; God existing in flesh; true life in death; both of Mary and of God; first possible and then impossible,—even Jesus Christ our Lord.

But some most worthless persons are in the habit of carrying about the name [of Jesus Christ] in wicked guile, while yet they practice things unworthy of God, and hold opinions contrary to the doctrine of Christ, to their own destruction, and that of those who give credit to them, whom you must avoid as ye would wild beasts. For "the righteous man who avoids them is saved forever; but the destruction of the ungodly is sudden, and a subject of rejoicing." For "they are dumb dogs, that cannot bark," raving mad, and biting secretly, against whom ye must be on your guard, since they labor under an incurable disease. But our Physician is the only true God, the unbegotten and unapproachable, the Lord of all, the Father and Begetter of the only-begotten Son. We have also as a Physician the Lord our God, Jesus the Christ, the only-begotten Son and Word, before time began, but who afterwards became also man, of Mary the virgin. For "the Word was made flesh." Being incorporeal, He was in the body; being impassible, He was in a passible body; being immortal, He was in a mortal body; being life, He became subject to corruption, that He might free our souls from death and corruption, and heal them, and might restore them to health, when they were diseased with ungodliness and wicked lusts.

Chapter VIII.—Renewed praise of the Ephesians.

Let not then any one deceive you, as indeed ye are not deceived, inasmuch as ye are wholly devoted to God. For since there is no strife raging among you which might distress you, ye are certainly living in accordance with God's will. I am far inferior to you, and require to be sanctified by your Church of Ephesus, so renowned throughout the world. They that are carnal cannot do those things which are spiritual, nor they that are spiritual the things which are carnal; even as faith cannot do the works of unbelief, nor unbelief the works of faith. But even those things which ye do according to the flesh are spiritual; for ye do all things in Jesus Christ. Let not then any one deceive you, as indeed ye are not deceived; for ye are wholly devoted to God. For when there is no evil desire within you, which might defile and torment you, then do ye live in accordance with the will of God, and are [the servants] of Christ. Cast you out that which defiles you, who are of the most holy Church of the Ephesians, which is so famous and celebrated throughout the world. They that are carnal cannot do those things which are spiritual, nor they that are spiritual the things which are carnal; even as faith cannot do the works of unbelief, nor unbelief the works of faith. But ye, being full of the Holy Spirit, do nothing according to the flesh, but all things according to the Spirit. Ye are complete in Christ Jesus, "who is the Savior of all men, especially of them that believe."

Chapter IX.—Ye have given no heed to false teachers.

Nevertheless, I have heard of some who have passed on from this to you, having false doctrine, whom ye did not suffer to sow among you, but stopped your ears, that ye might not receive those things which were sown by them, as being stones of the temple of the Father, prepared for the building of God the Father, and drawn up on high by the instrument of Jesus Christ, which is the cross, making use of the Holy Spirit as a rope, while your faith was the means by which you ascended, and your love the way which led up to God. Ye, therefore, as well as all your fellow-travelers, are God-bearers, temple-bearers, Christ bearers, bearers of holiness, adorned in all respects with the commandments of Jesus Christ, in whom also I exult that I have been thought worthy, by means of this Epistle, to converse and rejoice with you, because with respect to your Christian life ye love nothing but God only.

Nevertheless, I have heard of some who have passed in among you, holding the wicked doctrine of the strange and evil spirit; to whom ye did not allow entrance to sow their tares, but stopped your ears that ye might not receive that error which was proclaimed by them, as being persuaded that that spirit which deceives the people does not speak the things of Christ, but his own, for he is a lying spirit. But the Holy Spirit does not speak His own things, but those of Christ, and that not from himself, but from the Lord; even as the Lord also announced to us the things that He received from the Father. For, says He, "the word which ye hear is not Mine, but the Father's, who sent Me." And says He of the Holy Spirit, "He shall not speak of Himself, but whatsoever things He shall hear from Me." And He says of Himself to the Father, "I have," says He, "glorified Thee upon the earth; I have finished the work which, Thou gives Me; I have manifested Thy name to men." And of the Holy Ghost, "He shall glorify Me, for He receives of Mine." But the spirit of deceit preaches himself, and speaks his own things, for he seeks to please himself. He glorifies himself, for he is full of arrogance. He is lying, fraudulent, soothing, flattering, treacherous, rhapsodical, trifling, inharmonious, verbose, sordid, and timorous. From his power Jesus Christ will deliver you, who has founded you upon the rock, as being chosen stones, well fitted for the divine edifice of the Father, and who are raised up on high by Christ, who was crucified for you, making use of the Holy Spirit as a rope, and being borne up by faith, while exalted by love from earth to heaven, walking in company with those that are undefiled. For, says [the Scripture], "Blessed are the undefiled in the way, who walk in the law of the Lord." Now the way is unerring, namely, Jesus Christ. For, says He, "I am the way and the life." And this way leads to the Father. For "no man," says He, "cometh to the Father but by Me." Blessed, then, are ye who are God-bearers, spirit-bearers, temple-bearers, bearers of holiness, adorned in all respects with the commandments of Jesus Christ, being "a royal priesthood, a holy nation, a peculiar people," on whose account I rejoice exceedingly, and have had the privilege, by this Epistle, of conversing with "the saints which are at Ephesus, the faithful in Christ Jesus." I rejoice, therefore, over you, that ye do not give heed to vanity, and love nothing according to the flesh, but according to God.

Chapter X.—Exhortations to prayer, humility, etc.

And pray you without ceasing in behalf of other men. For there is in them hope of repentance that they may attain to God. See, then, that they be instructed by your works, if in no other way. Be ye meek in response to their wrath, humble in opposition to their boasting: to their blasphemies return your prayers; in contrast to their error, be ye steadfast in the faith; and for their cruelty, manifest your gentleness. While we take care not to imitate their conduct, let us be found their brethren in all true kindness; and let us seek to be followers of the Lord (who ever more unjustly treated, more destitute, more condemned?), that so no plant of the devil may be found in you, but ye may remain in all holiness and sobriety in Jesus Christ, both with respect to the flesh and spirit.

And pray you without ceasing in behalf of other men; for there is hope of the repentance, that they may attain to God. For "cannot he that falls arise again, and he that goes astray return?" Permit them, then, to be instructed by you. Be ye therefore the ministers of God, and the mouth of Christ. For thus saith the Lord, "If ye take forth the precious from the vile, ye shall be as my mouth." Be ye humble in response to their wrath; oppose to their blasphemies your earnest prayers; while they go astray, stand ye steadfast in the faith. Conquer ye their harsh temper by gentleness, their passion by meekness. For "blessed are the meek;" and Moses was meek above all men; and David was exceeding meek. Wherefore Paul exhorts as follows: "The servant of the Lord must not strive, but be gentle towards all men, apt to teach, patient, in meekness instructing those that oppose themselves." Do not seek to avenge yourselves on those that injure you, for says [the Scripture], "If I have returned evil to those who returned evil to me." Let us make them brethren by our kindness. For say you to those that hate you, Ye are our brethren, that the name of the Lord may be glorified. And let us imitate the Lord, "who, when He was reviled, reviled not again;" when He was crucified, He answered not; "when He suffered, He threatened not;" but prayed for His enemies, "Father, forgive them; they know not what they do." If anyone, the more he is injured, displays the more patience, blessed is he. If anyone is defrauded, if anyone is despised, for the name of the Lord, he truly is the servant of Christ. Take heed that no plant of the devil be found among you, for such a plant is bitter and salt. "Watch ye, and be ye sober," in Christ Jesus.

Chapter XI.—An exhortation to fear God, etc.

The last times are come upon us. Let us therefore be of a reverent spirit, and fear the long-suffering of God, that it tend not to our condemnation. For let us either stand in awe of the wrath to come, or show regard for the grace which is at present displayed— one of two things. Only [in one way or another] let us be found in Christ Jesus unto the true life. Apart from Him, let nothing attract you, for whom I bear about these bonds, these spiritual jewels, by which may I arise through your prayers, of which I entreat I may always be a partaker, that I may be found in the lot of the Christians of Ephesus, who have always been of the same mind with the apostles through the power of Jesus Christ.

The last times are come upon us. Let us therefore be of a reverent spirit, and fear the long-suffering of God, lest we despise the riches of His goodness and forbearance. For let us either fear the wrath to come, or let us love the present joy in the life that now is; and let our present and true joy be only this, to be found in Christ Jesus, that we may truly live. Do not at any time desire so much as even to breathe apart from Him. For He is my hope; He is my boast; He is my never-failing riches, on whose account I bear about with me these bonds from Syria to Rome, these spiritual jewels, in which may I be perfected through your prayers, and become a partaker of the sufferings of Christ, and have fellowship with Him in His death, His resurrection from the dead, and His everlasting life. May I attain to this, so that I may be found in the lot of the Christians of Ephesus, who have always had intercourse with the apostles by the power of Jesus Christ, with Paul, and John, and Timothy the most faithful.

Chapter XII.—Praise of the Ephesians.

I know both who I am, and to whom I write. I am a condemned man, ye have been the objects of mercy; I am subject to danger, ye are established in safety. Ye are the persons through whom those pass that are cut off for the sake of God. Ye are initiated into the mysteries of the

Gospel with Paul, the holy, the martyred, the deservedly most happy, at whose feet may I be found, when I shall attain to God; who in all his Epistles makes mention of you in Christ Jesus.

I know both who I am, and to whom I write. I am the very insignificant Ignatius, who have my lot with those who are exposed to danger and condemnation. But ye have been the objects of mercy, and are established in Christ. I am one delivered over [to death], but the least of all those that have been cut off for the sake of Christ, "from the blood of righteous Abel" to the blood of Ignatius. Ye are initiated into the mysteries of the Gospel with Paul, the holy, the martyred, inasmuch as he was "a chosen vessel;" at whose feet may I be found, and at the feet of the rest of the saints, when I shall attain to Jesus Christ, who is always mindful of you in His prayers.

Chapter XIII.—Exhortation to meet together frequently for the worship of God.

Take heed, then, often to come together to give thanks to God, and show forth His praise. For when ye assemble frequently in the same place, the powers of Satan are destroyed, and the destruction at which he aims is prevented by the unity of your faith. Nothing is more precious than peace, by which all war, both in heaven and earth, is brought to an end. Take heed, then, often to come together to give thanks to God, and show forth His praise. For when ye come frequently together in the same place, the powers of Satan are destroyed, and his "fiery darts" urging to sin fall back ineffectual. For your concord and harmonious faith prove his destruction, and the torment of his assistants. Nothing is better than that peace which is according to Christ, by which all war, both of aërial and terrestrial spirits, is brought to an end. "For we wrestle not against blood and flesh, but against principalities and powers, and against the rulers of the darkness of this world, against spiritual wickedness in heavenly places."

Chapter XIV.—Exhortations to faith and love.

None of these things is hid from you, if ye perfectly possess that faith and love towards Christ Jesus which are the beginning and the end of life. For the beginning is faith, and the end is love. Now these two, being inseparably connected together, are of God, while all other things which are requisite for a holy life follow after them. No man [truly] making a profession of faith sinned; nor does he that possesses love hate anyone. The tree is made manifest by its fruit; so those that profess themselves to be Christians shall be recognized by their conduct. For there is not now a demand for mere profession, but that a man be found continuing in the power of faith to the end.

Wherefore none of the devices of the devil shall be hidden from you, if, like Paul, ye perfectly possess that faith and love towards Christ which are the beginning and the end of life. The beginning of life is faith, and the end is love. And these two being inseparably connected together, do perfect the man of God; while all other things which are requisite to a holy life follow after them. No man making a profession of faith ought to sin, nor one possessed of love to hate his brother. For He that said, "Thou shalt love the Lord thy God," said also, "and thy neighbor as thyself." Those that profess themselves to be Christ's are known not only by what they say, but by what they practice. "For the tree is known by its fruit."

Chapter XV.—Exhortation to confess Christ by silence as well as speech.

It is better for a man to be silent and be [a Christian], than to talk and not to be one. It is good to teach, if he who speaks also acts. There is then one Teacher, who spoke and it was done; while even those things which He did in silence are worthy of the Father. He who possesses the word of Jesus, is truly able to hear even His very silence, that he may be perfect, and may both act as he speaks, and be recognized by his silence. There is nothing which is hid from God, but our very secrets are near to Him. Let us therefore do all things as those who have Him dwelling in us, that we may be His temples, and He may be in us as our God, which indeed He is, and will manifest Himself before our faces. Wherefore we justly love Him.

It is better for a man to be silent and be [a Christian], than to talk and not to be one. "The kingdom of God is not in word, but in power." Men "believe with the heart, and confess with the mouth," the one "unto righteousness," the other "unto salvation." It is good to teach, if he who speaks also acts. For he who shall both "do and teach, the same shall be great in the kingdom." Our Lord and God, Jesus Christ, the Son of the living God, first did and then taught, as Luke testifies, "whose praise is in the Gospel through all the Churches." There is nothing which is hid from the Lord, but our very secrets are near to Him. Let us therefore do all things as those who have Him dwelling in us, that we may be His temples, and He may be in us as God. Let Christ speak in us, even as He did in Paul. Let the Holy Spirit teach us to speak the things of Christ in like manner as He did.

Chapter XVI.—The fate of false teachers.

Do not err, my brethren. Those that corrupt families shall not inherit the kingdom of God. If, then, those who do this as respects the flesh have suffered death, how much more shall this be the case with anyone who corrupts by wicked doctrine the faith of God, for which Jesus Christ was crucified! Such a one becoming defiled [in this way], shall go away into everlasting fire, and so shall everyone that hearkens unto him.

Do not err, my brethren. Those that corrupt families shall not inherit the kingdom of God. And if those that corrupt mere human families are condemned to death, how much more shall those suffer everlasting punishment who endeavor to corrupt the Church of Christ, for which the Lord Jesus, the only-begotten Son of God, endured the cross, and submitted to death! Whosoever, "being waxen fat," and "become gross," sets at naught His doctrine, shall go into hell. In like manner, every one that has received from God the power of distinguishing, and yet follows an unskillful shepherd, and receives a false opinion for the truth, shall be punished. "What communion hath light with darkness? Or Christ with Belial? Or what portion hath he that believeth with an infidel? Or the temple of God with idols?" And in like manner say I, what communion hath truth with falsehood? Or righteousness with unrighteousness? Or true doctrine with that which is false?

Chapter XVII.—Beware of false doctrines.

For this end did the Lord suffer the ointment to be poured upon His head, that He might breathe immortality into His Church. Be not ye anointed with the bad odor of the doctrine of the prince of this world; let him not lead you away captive from the life which is set before you. And why are we not all prudent, since we have received the knowledge of God, which is Jesus Christ? Why do we foolishly perish, not recognizing the gift which the Lord has of a truth sent to us?

For this end did the Lord suffer the ointment to be poured upon His head, that His Church might breathe forth immortality. For saith [the Scripture], "Thy name is as ointment poured forth; therefore have the virgins loved Thee; they have drawn Thee; at the odor of Thine ointments we will run after Thee." Let no one be anointed with the bad odor of the doctrine of [the prince of] this world; let not the holy Church of God be led captive by his subtlety, as was the first woman. Why do we not, as gifted with reason, act wisely? When we had received from Christ, and had grafted in us the faculty of judging concerning God, why do we fall headlong into ignorance? And why, through a careless neglect of acknowledging the gift which we have received, do we foolishly perish?

Chapter XVIII.—The glory of the cross.

Let my spirit be counted as nothing for the sake of the cross, which is a stumbling block to those that do not believe, but to us salvation and life eternal. "Where is the wise man? Where the disputer?" Where is the boasting of those who are styled prudent? For our God, Jesus Christ, was, according to the appointment of God, conceived in the womb by Mary, of the seed of David, but by the Holy Ghost. He was born and baptized, that by His passion He might purify the water.

The cross of Christ is indeed a stumbling-block to those that do not believe, but to the believing it is salvation and life eternal. "Where is the wise man? Where the disputer?" Where is the boasting of those who are called mighty? For the Son of God, who was begotten before time began, and established all things according to the will of the Father, He was conceived in the womb of Mary, according to the appointment of God, of the seed of David, and by the Holy Ghost. For says [the Scripture], "Behold, a virgin shall be with child, and shall bring forth a son, and He shall be called Immanuel." He was born and was baptized by John, that He might ratify the institution committed to that prophet.

Chapter XIX.—Three celebrated mysteries.

Now the virginity of Mary was hidden from the prince of this world, as was also her offspring, and the death of the Lord; three mysteries of renown, which were wrought in silence by God. How, then, was He manifested to the world? A star shone forth in heaven above all the other stars, the light of which was inexpressible, while its novelty struck men with astonishment. And all the rest of the stars, with the sun and moon, formed a chorus to this star, and its light was exceedingly great above them all. And there was agitation felt as to whence this new spectacle came, so unlike to everything else [in the heavens]. Hence every kind of magic was destroyed, and every bond of wickedness disappeared; ignorance was removed, and the old kingdom abolished, God Himself being manifested in human form for the renewal of eternal life. And now that took a beginning which had been prepared by God. Henceforth all things were in a state of tumult, because He meditated the abolition of death.

Now the virginity of Mary was hidden from the prince of this world, as was also her offspring, and the death of the Lord; three mysteries of renown, which were wrought in silence, but have been revealed to us. A star shone forth in heaven above all that were before it, and its light was inexpressible, while its novelty struck men with astonishment. And all the rest of the stars, with the sun and moon, formed a chorus to this star. It far exceeded them all in brightness, and agitation was felt as to whence this new spectacle [proceeded]. Hence worldly wisdom became folly; conjuration was seen to be mere trifling; and magic became utterly ridiculous. Every law of wickedness vanished away; the darkness of ignorance was dispersed; and tyrannical authority was destroyed, God being manifested as a man, and man displaying power as God. But neither was the former a mere imagination, nor did the second imply a bare humanity; but the one was absolutely true, and the other an economical arrangement. Now that received a beginning which was perfected by God. Henceforth all things were in a state of tumult, because He meditated the abolition of death.

Chapter XX.—Promise of another letter.

If Jesus Christ shall graciously permit me through your prayers, and if it be His will, I shall, in a second little work which I will write to you, make further manifest to you [the nature of] the dispensation of which I have begun [to treat], with respect to the new man, Jesus Christ, in His faith and in His love, in His suffering and in His resurrection. Especially [will I do this] if the Lord make known to me that ye come together man by man in common through grace, individually, in one faith, and in Jesus Christ, who was of the seed of David according to the flesh, being both the Son of man and the Son of God, so that ye obey the bishop and the presbytery with an undivided mind, breaking one and the same bread, which is the medicine of immortality, and the antidote to prevent us from dying, but [which causes] that we should live forever in Jesus Christ.

Chapter XX.—Exhortations to steadfastness and unity.

Stand fast, brethren, in the faith of Jesus Christ, and in His love, in His passion, and in His resurrection. Do ye all come together in common, and individually, through grace, in one faith of God the Father, and of Jesus Christ His only-begotten Son, and "the firstborn of every creature," but of the seed of David according to the flesh, being under the guidance of the Comforter, in obedience to the bishop and the presbytery with an undivided mind, breaking one and the same bread, which is the medicine of immortality, and the antidote which prevents us from dying, but a cleansing remedy driving away evil, [which causes] that we should live in God through Jesus Christ.

Chapter XXI.—Conclusion.

My soul be for yours and theirs whom, for the

The Epistles of St. Ignatius

honor of God, ye have sent to Smyrna; whence also I write to you, giving thanks unto the Lord, and loving Polycarp even as I do you. Remember me, as Jesus Christ also remembered you. Pray ye for the Church which is in Syria, whence I am led bound to Rome, being the last of the faithful who are there, even as I have been thought worthy to be chosen to show forth the honor of God. Farewell in God the Father, and in Jesus Christ, our common hope.

My soul be for yours and theirs whom, for the honor of God, ye have sent to Smyrna; whence also I write to you, giving thanks to the Lord, and loving Polycarp even as I do you. Remember me, as Jesus Christ also remembers you, who is blessed for evermore. Pray you for the Church of Antioch which is in Syria, whence I am led bound to Rome, being the last of the faithful that are there, who yet have been thought worthy to carry these chains to the honor of God. Fare ye well in God the Father, and the Lord Jesus Christ, our common hope, and in the Holy Ghost. Fare ye well. Amen. Grace [be with you].

The Epistle of Ignatius to the Magnesians Shorter and Longer Versions

Ignatius, who is also called Theophorus, to the [Church] blessed in the grace of God the Father, in Jesus Christ our Savior, in whom I salute the Church which is at Magnesia, near the Mæander, and wish it abundance of happiness in God the Father, and in Jesus Christ.

Ignatius, who is also called Theophorus, to the [Church] blessed in the grace of God the Father, in Jesus Christ our Savior, in whom I salute the Church which is at

Magnesia, near the Mæander, and wish it abundance of happiness in God the Father, and in Jesus Christ, our Lord, in whom may you have abundance of happiness.

Chapter I.—Reason of writing the epistle.

Having been informed of your godly love, so well-ordered, I rejoiced greatly, and determined to commune with you in the faith of Jesus Christ. For as one who has been thought worthy of the most honorable of all names, in those bonds which I bear about, I commend the Churches, in which I pray for a union both of the flesh and spirit of Jesus Christ, the constant source of our life, and of faith and love, to which nothing is to be preferred, but especially of Jesus and the Father, in whom, if we endure all the assaults of the prince of this world, and escape them, we shall enjoy God.

Having been informed of your godly love, so well-ordered, I rejoiced greatly, and determined to commune with you in the faith of Jesus Christ. For as one who has been thought worthy of a divine and desirable name, in those bonds which I bear about, I commend the Churches, in which I pray for a union both of the flesh and spirit of Jesus Christ, "who is the Savior of all men, but specially of them that believe;" by whose blood ye were redeemed; by whom ye have known God, or rather have been known by Him; in whom enduring, ye shall escape all the assaults of this world: for "He is faithful, who will not suffer you to be tempted above that which ye are able."

Chapter II.—I rejoice in your messengers.

Since, then, I have had the privilege of seeing you,

through Damas your most worthy bishop, and through your worthy presbyters Bassus and Apollonius, and through my fellow servant the deacon Sotio, whose friendship may I ever enjoy, inasmuch as he is subject to the bishop as to the grace of God, and to the presbytery as to the law of Jesus Christ, [I now write to you]. Since, then, I have had the privilege of seeing you, through Damas your most worthy bishop, and through your worthy presbyters Bassus and Apollonius, and through my fellow-servant the deacon Sotio, whose friendship may I ever enjoy, inasmuch as he, by the grace of God, is subject to the bishop and presbytery, in the law of Jesus Christ, [I now write to you].

Chapter III.—Honor your youthful bishop.

Now it becomes you also not to treat your bishop too familiarly on account of his youth, but to yield him all reverence, having respect to the power of God the Father, as I have known even holy presbyters do, not judging rashly, from the manifest youthful appearance [of their bishop], but as being themselves prudent in God, submitting to him, or rather not to him, but to the Father of Jesus Christ, the bishop of us all. It is therefore fitting that you should, after no hypocritical fashion, obey [your bishop], in honor of Him who has willed us [so to do], since he that does not so deceives not [by such conduct] the bishop that is visible, but seeks to mock Him that is invisible. And all such conduct has reference not to man, but to God, who knows all secrets. Now it becomes you also not to despise the age of your bishop, but to yield him all reverence, according to the will of God the Father, as I have known even holy presbyters do, not having regard to the manifest youth [of their bishop], but to his knowledge in God; inasmuch as "not the ancient are [necessarily] wise, nor do the aged understand prudence; but there is a spirit in men." For Daniel the wise, at twelve years of age, became possessed of the divine Spirit, and convicted the elders, who in vain carried their grey hairs, of being false accusers, and of lusting after the beauty of another man's wife. Samuel also, when he was but a little child, reproved Eli, who was ninety years old, for giving honor to his sons rather than to God. In like manner, Jeremiah also received this message from God, "Say not, I am a child." Solomon too, and Josiah, [exemplified the same thing.] The former, being made king at twelve years of age, gave that terrible and difficult judgment in the case of the two women concerning their children. The latter, coming to the throne when eight years old cast down the altars and temples [of the idols], and burned down the groves, for they were dedicated to demons, and not to God. And he slew the false priests, as the corrupters and deceivers of men, and not the worshippers of the Deity. Wherefore youth is not to be despised when it is devoted to God. But he is to be despised who is of a wicked mind, although he be old, and full of wicked days. Timothy the Christ-bearer was young, but hear what his teacher writes to him: "Let no man despise thy youth, but be thou an example of the believers in word and in conduct." It is becoming, therefore, that ye also should be obedient to your bishop, and contradict him in nothing; for it is a fearful thing to contradict any such person. For no one does [by such conduct] deceive him that is visible, but does [in reality] seek to mock Him that is invisible, who, however, cannot be mocked by anyone. And every such act has respect not to man, but to God. For God says to Samuel, "They have not mocked thee, but Me." And Moses declares, "For their murmuring is not against us, but against the Lord God." No one of those has, [in fact,] remained unpunished, who rose up against their superiors. For Dathan and Abiram did not speak against the law, but against Moses, and were cast down alive into Hades. Korah also, and the two hundred and fifty who conspired with him against Aaron, were destroyed by fire. Absalom, again, who had slain his brother, became suspended on a tree, and had his evil-designing heart thrust through with darts. In like manner was Abeddadan beheaded for the same reason. Uzziah, when he presumed to oppose the priests and the priesthood, was smitten with leprosy. Saul also was dishonored, because he did not wait for Samuel the high priest. It behooves you, therefore, also to reverence your superiors.

Chapter IV.—Some wickedly act independently of the bishop.

It is fitting, then, not only to be called Christians, but to be so in reality: as some indeed give one the title of bishop, but do all things without him. Now such persons seem to me to be not possessed of a good conscience, seeing they are not steadfastly gathered together according to the commandment.

It is fitting, then, not only to be called Christians, but to be so in reality. For it is not the being called so, but the being really so, that renders a man blessed. To those who indeed talk of the bishop, but do all things without him, will He who is the true and first Bishop, and the only High Priest by nature, declare, "Why call you Me Lord, and do not the things which I say?" For such persons seem to me not possessed of a good conscience, but to be simply dissemblers and hypocrites.

Chapter V.—Death is the fate of all such.

Seeing, then, all things have an end, these two things are simultaneously set before us—death and life; and every one shall go unto his own place. For as there are two kinds of coins, the one of God, the other of the world, and each of these has its special character stamped upon it, [so is it also here.] The unbelieving are of this world; but the believing have, in love, the character of God the Father by Jesus Christ, by whom, if we are not in readiness to die into His passion, His life is not in us.

Seeing, then, all things have an end, and there is set before us life upon our observance [of God's precepts], but death as the result of disobedience, and everyone, according to the choice he makes, shall go to his own place, let us flee from death, and make choice of life. For I remark, that two different characters are found among men—the one true coin, the other spurious. The truly devout man is the right kind of coin, stamped by God Himself. The ungodly man, again, is false coin, unlawful, spurious, counterfeit, wrought not by God, but by the devil. I do not mean to say that there are two different human natures, but that there is one humanity, sometimes belonging to God, and sometimes to the devil. If anyone is truly religious, he is a man of God; but if he is irreligious, he is a man of the devil, made such, not by nature, but by his own choice. The unbelieving bear the image of the prince of wickedness. The believing possess the image of their Prince, God the Father, and Jesus Christ, through whom, if we are not in readiness to die for the truth into His passion, His life is not in us.

Chapter VI.—Preserve harmony.

Since therefore I have, in the persons before mentioned, beheld the whole multitude of you in faith and love, I exhort you to study to do all things with a divine harmony, while your bishop presides in the place of God, and your presbyters in the place of the assembly of the apostles, along with your deacons, who are most dear to me, and are entrusted with the ministry of Jesus Christ, who was with the Father before the beginning of time, and in the end was revealed. Do ye all then, imitating the same divine conduct, pay respect to one another, and let no one look upon his neighbor after the flesh, but do ye continually love each other in Jesus Christ. Let nothing exist among you that may divide you; but be ye united with your bishop, and those that preside over you, as a type and evidence of your immortality.

Since therefore I have, in the persons before mentioned, beheld the whole multitude of you in faith and love, I exhort you to study to do all things with a divine harmony, while your bishop presides in the place of God, and your presbyters in the place of the assembly of the apostles, along with your deacons, who are most dear to me, and are entrusted with the ministry of Jesus Christ. He, being begotten by the Father before the beginning of time, was God the Word, the only-begotten Son, and remains the same forever; for "of His kingdom there shall be no end," says Daniel the prophet. Let us all therefore love one another in harmony, and let no one look upon his neighbor according to the flesh, but in Christ Jesus. Let nothing exist among you which may divide you; but be ye united with your bishop, being through him subject to God in Christ.

Chapter VII.—Do nothing without the bishop and presbyters.

As therefore the Lord did nothing without the Father, being united to Him, neither by Himself nor by the apostles, so neither do you anything without the bishop and presbyters. Neither endeavor that anything appear reasonable and proper to yourselves apart; but being come together into the same place, let there be one prayer, one supplication, one mind, one hope, in love and in joy undefiled. There is one Jesus Christ, than whom nothing is more excellent. Do ye therefore all run together as into one temple of God, as to one altar, as to one Jesus Christ, who came forth from one Father, and is with and has gone to one.

As therefore the Lord does nothing without the Father, for says He, "I can of mine own self do nothing," so do ye, neither presbyter, nor deacon, nor layman, do anything without the bishop. Nor let anything appear commendable to you which is destitute of his approval. For every such thing is sinful, and opposed [to the will of] God. Do ye all come together into the same place for prayer. Let there be one common supplication, one mind, one hope, with faith unblameable in Christ Jesus, than which nothing is more excellent. Do ye all, as one man, run together into the temple of God, as unto one altar, to one Jesus Christ, the High Priest of the unbegotten God.

Chapter VIII.—Caution against false doctrines.

Be not deceived with strange doctrines, nor with old fables, which are unprofitable. For if we still live according to the Jewish law, we acknowledge that we have not received grace. For the divinest prophets lived according to Christ Jesus. On this account also they were persecuted, being inspired by His grace to fully convince the unbelieving that there is one God, who has manifested Himself by Jesus Christ His Son, who is His eternal Word, not proceeding forth from silence, and who in all things pleased Him that sent Him.

Be not deceived with strange doctrines, "nor give heed to fables and endless genealogies," and things in which the Jews make their boast. "Old things are passed away: behold, all things have become new." For if we still live according to the Jewish law, and the circumcision of the flesh, we deny that we have received grace. For the divinest prophets lived according to Jesus Christ. On this account also they were persecuted, being inspired by grace to fully convince the unbelieving that there is one God, the Almighty, who has manifested Himself by Jesus Christ His Son, who is His Word, not spoken, but essential. For He is not the voice of an articulate utterance, but a substance begotten by divine power, who has in all things pleased Him that sent Him.

Chapter IX.—Let us live with Christ.

If, therefore, those who were brought up in the ancient order of things have come to the possession of a new hope, no longer observing the Sabbath, but living in the observance of the Lord's Day, on which also our life has sprung up again by Him and by His death—whom some deny, by which mystery we have obtained faith, and therefore endure, that we may be found the disciples of Jesus Christ, our only Master—how shall we be able to live apart from Him, whose disciples the prophets themselves in the Spirit did wait for Him as their Teacher? And therefore He whom they rightly waited for, being come, raised them from the dead. If, then, those who were conversant with the ancient Scriptures came to newness of hope, expecting the coming of Christ, as the Lord teaches us when He says, "If ye had believed Moses, ye would have believed Me, for he wrote of Me;" and again, "Your father Abraham rejoiced to see My day, and he saw it, and was glad; for before Abraham was, I am;" how shall we be able to live without Him? The prophets were His servants, and foresaw Him by the Spirit, and waited for Him as their Teacher, and expected Him as their Lord and Savior, saying, "He will come and save us." Let us therefore no longer keep the Sabbath after the Jewish manner, and rejoice in days of idleness; for "he that does not work, let him not eat." For say the [holy] oracles, "In the sweat of thy face shalt thou eat thy bread." But let every one of you keep the Sabbath after a spiritual manner, rejoicing in meditation on the law, not in relaxation of the body, admiring the workmanship of God, and not eating things prepared the day before, nor using lukewarm drinks, and walking within a prescribed space, nor finding delight in dancing and plaudits which have no sense in them. And after the observance of the Sabbath, let every friend of Christ keep the Lord's Day as a festival, the resurrection-day, the queen and chief of all the days [of the week]. Looking forward to this, the prophet declared, "To the end, for the eighth day," on which our life both sprang up again, and the victory over death was obtained in Christ, whom the children of perdition, the enemies of the Savior, deny, "whose god is their belly, who mind earthly things," who are "lovers of pleasure, and not lovers of God, having a form of godliness, but denying the power thereof." These make merchandise of Christ, corrupting His word, and giving up Jesus to sale: they are corrupters of women, and covetous of other men's possessions, swallowing up wealth insatiably; from whom may ye be delivered by the mercy of God through our Lord Jesus Christ!

Chapter X.—Beware of Judaizing.

Let us not, therefore, be insensible to His kindness. For were He to reward us according to our works, we should cease to be. Therefore, having become His disciples, let us learn to live according to the principles of Christianity. For whosoever is called by any other name besides this, is not of God. Lay aside, therefore, the evil, the old, the sour leaven, and be ye changed into the new leaven, which is Jesus Christ. Be ye salted in Him, lest anyone among you should be corrupted, since by your savor ye shall be convicted. It is absurd to profess Christ Jesus, and to Judaize. For Christianity did not embrace Judaism, but Judaism Christianity, that so every tongue which believeth might be gathered together to God.

Let us not, therefore, be insensible to His kindness. For were He to reward us according to our works, we should cease to be. For "if Thou, Lord, shalt mark iniquities, O Lord, who shall stand?" Let us therefore prove ourselves worthy of that name which we have received. For whosoever is called by any other name besides this, he is not of God; for he has not received the prophecy which speaks thus concerning us: "The people shall be called by a new name, which the Lord shall name them, and shall be a holy people." This was first fulfilled in Syria; for "the disciples were called Christians at Antioch," when Paul and Peter were laying the foundations of the Church. Lay aside, therefore, the evil, the old, the corrupt leaven, and be ye changed into the new leaven of grace. Abide in Christ, that the stranger may not have dominion over you. It is absurd to speak of Jesus Christ with the tongue, and to cherish in the mind a Judaism which has now come to an end. For where there is Christianity there cannot be Judaism. For Christ is one, in whom every nation that believes, and every tongue that confesses, is gathered unto God. And those that were of a stony heart have become the children of Abraham, the friend of God; and in his seed all those have been blessed who were ordained to eternal life in Christ.

Chapter XI.—I write these things to warn you.

These things [I address to you], my beloved, not that I know any of you to be in such a state; but, as less than any of you, I desire to guard you beforehand, that ye fall not upon the hooks of vain doctrine, but that ye attain to full assurance in regard to the birth, and passion, and resurrection which took place in the time of the government of Pontius Pilate, being truly and certainly accomplished by Jesus Christ, who is our hope, from which may no one of you ever be turned aside.

These things [I address to you], my beloved, not that I know any of you to be in such a state; but, as less than any of you, I desire to guard you beforehand, that ye fall not upon the hooks of vain doctrine, but that you may rather attain to a full assurance in Christ, who was begotten by the Father before all ages, but was afterwards born of the Virgin Mary without any intercourse with man. He also lived a holy life, and healed every kind of sickness and disease among the people, and wrought signs and wonders for the benefit of men; and to those who had fallen into the error of polytheism He made known the one and only true God, His Father, and underwent the passion, and endured the cross at the hands of the Christ-killing Jews, under Pontius Pilate the governor and Herod the king. He also died, and rose again, and ascended into the heavens to Him that sent Him, and is sat down at His right hand, and shall come at the end of the world, with His Father's glory, to judge the living and the dead, and to render to everyone according to his works. He who knows these things with a full assurance, and believes them, is happy; even as ye are now the lovers of God and of Christ, in the full assurance of our hope, from which may no one of us ever be turned aside!

Chapter XII.—Ye are superior to me.

May I enjoy you in all respects, if indeed I be worthy! For though I am bound, I am not worthy to be compared to any of you that are at liberty. I know that ye are not puffed up, for ye have Jesus Christ in yourselves. And all the more when I commend you, I know that ye cherish modesty of spirit; as it is written, "The righteous man is his own accuser."

May I enjoy you in all respects, if indeed I be worthy! For though I am bound, I am not worthy to be compared to one of you that are at liberty. I know that ye are not puffed up, for ye have Jesus in yourselves. And all the more when I commend you, I know that ye cherish modesty of spirit; as it is written, "The righteous man is his own accuser;" and again, "Declare thou first thine iniquities, that thou mayest be justified;" and again, "When ye shall have done all things that are commanded you, say, We are unprofitable servants;" "for that which is highly esteemed among men is abomination in the sight of God." For says [the Scripture], "God be merciful to me a sinner." Therefore those great ones, Abraham and Job, styled themselves "dust and ashes" before God. And David says, "Who am I before Thee, O Lord, that Thou hast glorified me hitherto?" And Moses, who was "the meekest of all men," saith to God, "I am of a feeble voice, and of a slow tongue." Be ye therefore also of a humble spirit, that ye may be exalted; for "he that abases himself shall be exalted, and he that exalted himself shall be abased."

Chapter XIII.—Be established in faith and unity.

Study, therefore, to be established in the doctrines of the Lord and the apostles, that so all things, whatsoever ye do, may prosper both in the flesh and spirit; in faith and love; in the Son, and in the Father, and in the Spirit; in the beginning and in the end; with your most admirable bishop, and the well-compacted spiritual crown of your presbytery, and the deacons who are according to God. Be ye subject to the bishop, and to one another, as Jesus Christ to the Father, according to the flesh, and the apostles to Christ, and to the Father, and to the Spirit; that so there may be a union both fleshly and spiritual.

Study, therefore, to be established in the doctrines of the Lord and the apostles, that so all things, whatsoever ye do, may prosper, both in the flesh and spirit, in faith and love, with your most admirable bishop, and the well-compacted spiritual crown of your presbytery, and the deacons who are according to God. Be ye subject to the bishop, and to one another, as Christ to the Father, that there may be a unity according to God among you.

Chapter XIV.—Your prayers requested.

Knowing as I do that ye are full of God, I have but briefly exhorted you. Be mindful of me in your prayers, that I may attain to God; and of the Church which is in Syria, whence I am not worthy to derive my name: for I stand in need of your united prayer in God, and your love, that the Church which is in Syria may be deemed worthy of being refreshed by your Church.

Knowing as I do that ye are full of all good, I have but briefly exhorted you in the love of Jesus Christ. Be mindful of me in your prayers, that I may attain to God; and of the Church which is in Syria, of whom I am not worthy to be called bishop. For I stand in need of your united prayer in God, and of your love, that the Church which is in Syria may be deemed worthy, by your good order, of being edified in Christ.

Chapter XV.—Salutations.

The Ephesians from Smyrna (whence I also write to you), who are here for the glory of God, as ye also are, who have in all things refreshed me, salute you, along with Polycarp, the bishop of the Smyrnæans. The rest of the Churches, in honor of Jesus Christ, also salute you. Fare ye well in the harmony of God, ye who have obtained the inseparable Spirit, who is Jesus Christ.

The Ephesians from Smyrna (whence I also write to you), who are here for the glory of God, as ye also are, who have in all things refreshed me, salute you, as does also Polycarp. The rest of the Churches, in honor of Jesus Christ, also salute you. Fare ye well in harmony, ye who have obtained the inseparable Spirit, in Christ Jesus, by the will of God.

The Epistle of Ignatius to the Trallians Shorter and Longer Versions

Ignatius, who is also called Theophorus, to the holy Church which is at Tralles, in Asia, beloved of God, the Father of Jesus Christ, elect, and worthy of God, possessing peace through the flesh, and blood, and passion of Jesus Christ, who is our hope, through our rising again to Him, which also I salute in its fullness, and in the apostolical character, and wish abundance of happiness.

Ignatius, who is also called Theophorus, to the holy Church which is at Tralles, beloved by God the Father, and Jesus Christ, elect, and worthy of God, possessing peace through the flesh and Spirit of Jesus Christ, who is our hope, in His passion by the cross and death, and in His resurrection, which also I salute in its fullness, and in the apostolical character, and wish abundance of happiness.

Chapter I.—Acknowledgment of their excellence.

I know that ye possess an unblameable and sincere mind in patience, and that not only in present practice, but according to inherent nature, as Polybius your bishop has shown me, who has come to Smyrna by the will of God and Jesus Christ, and so sympathized in the joy which I, who am bound in Christ Jesus, possess, that I beheld your whole multitude in him. Having therefore received through him the testimony of your good-will, according to God, I gloried to find you, as I knew you were, the followers of God.

I know that ye possess an unblameable and sincere mind in patience, and that not only for present use, but as a permanent possession, as Polybius your bishop has shown me, who has come to Smyrna by the will of God the Father, and the Lord Jesus Christ, His Son, with the co-operation of the Spirit, and so sympathized in the joy which I, who am bound in Christ Jesus, possess, that I beheld your whole multitude in Him. Having therefore received through him the testimony of your good-will according to God, I gloried to find that you were the followers of Jesus Christ the Savior.

Chapter II.—Be subject to the bishop, etc.

For, since ye are subject to the bishop as to Jesus Christ, ye appear to me to live not after the manner of men, but according to Jesus Christ, who died for us, in order, by believing in His death, ye may escape from death. It is therefore necessary that, as ye indeed do, so without the bishop ye should do nothing, but should also be subject to the presbytery, as to the apostle of Jesus

Christ, who is our hope, in whom, if we live, we shall [at last] be found. It is fitting also that the deacons, as being [the ministers] of the mysteries of Jesus Christ, should in every respect be pleasing to all. For they are not ministers of meat and drink, but servants of the Church of God. They are bound, therefore, to avoid all grounds of accusation [against them], as they would do fire.

Be ye subject to the bishop as to the Lord, for "he watches for your souls, as one that shall give account to God." Wherefore also, ye appear to me to live not after the manner of men, but according to Jesus Christ, who died for us, in order that, by believing in His death, ye may by baptism be made partakers of His resurrection. It is therefore necessary, whatsoever things ye do, to do nothing without the bishop. And be ye subject also to the presbytery, as to the apostles of Jesus Christ, who is our hope, in whom, if we live, we shall be found in Him. It behooves you also, in every way, to please the deacons, who are [ministers] of the mysteries of Christ Jesus; for they are not ministers of meat and drink, but servants of the Church of God. They are bound, therefore, to avoid all grounds of accusation [against them], as they would a burning fire. Let them, then, prove themselves to be such.

Chapter III.—Honor the deacons, etc.

In like manner, let all reverence the deacons as an appointment of Jesus Christ, and the bishop as Jesus Christ, who is the Son of the Father, and the presbyters as the Sanhedrim of God, and assembly of the apostles. Apart from these, there is no Church. Concerning all this, I am persuaded that ye are of the same opinion. For I have received the manifestation of your love, and still have it with me, in your bishop, whose very appearance is highly instructive, and his meekness of itself a power; whom I imagine even the ungodly must reverence, seeing they are also pleased that I do not spare myself. But shall I, when permitted to write on this point, reach such a height of self-esteem, that though being a condemned man, I should issue commands to you as if I were an apostle?

And do ye reverence them as Christ Jesus, of whose place they are the keepers, even as the bishop is the representative of the Father of all things, and the presbyters are the Sanhedrim of God, and assembly of the apostles of Christ. Apart from these there is no elect Church, no congregation of holy ones, no assembly of saints. I am persuaded that ye also are of this opinion. For I have received the manifestation of your love, and still have it with me, in your bishop, whose very appearance is highly instructive, and his meekness of itself a power; whom I imagine even the ungodly must reverence. Loving you as I do, I avoid writing in any severer strain to you, that I may not seem harsh to any, or wanting [in tenderness]. I am indeed bound for the sake of Christ, but I am not yet worthy of Christ. But when I am perfected, perhaps I shall then become so. I do not issue orders like an apostle.

Chapter IV.—I have need of humility.

I have great knowledge in God, but I restrain myself, lest, I should perish through boasting. For now it is needful for me to be the more fearful; and not give heed to those that puff me up. For they that speak to me [in the way of commendation] scourge me. For I do indeed desire to suffer, but I know not if I be worthy to do so. For this longing, though it is not manifest to many, all the more vehemently assails me. I therefore have need of meekness, by which the prince of this world is brought to naught.

But I measure myself, that I may not perish through boasting: but it is good to glory in the Lord. And even though I were established in things pertaining to God, yet then would it befit me to be the more fearful, and not give heed to those that vainly puff me up. For those that commend me scourge me. [I do indeed desire to suffer], but I know not if I be worthy to do so. For the envy of the wicked one is not visible to many, but it wars against me. I therefore have need of meekness, by which the devil, the prince of this world, is brought to naught.

Chapter V.—I will not teach you profound doctrines.

Am I not able to write to you of heavenly things? But I fear to do so, lest I should inflict injury on you who are but babes [in Christ]. Pardon me in this respect, lest, as not being able to receive [such doctrines], ye should be strangled by them. For even I, though I am bound [for Christ], yet am not on that account able to understand heavenly things, and the places of the angels, and their gatherings under their respective princes, things visible and invisible. Without reference to such abstruse subjects, I am still but a learner [in other respects]; for many things are wanting to us, that we come not short of God.

For might not I write to you things more full of mystery? But I fear to do so, lest I should inflict injury on you who are but babes [in Christ]. Pardon me in this respect, lest, as not being able to receive their weighty import, ye should be strangled by them. For even I, though I am bound [for Christ], and am able to understand heavenly things, the angelic orders, and the different sorts of angels and hosts, the distinctions between powers and dominions, and the diversities between thrones and authorities, the mightiness of the Æons, and the pre-eminence of the cherubim and seraphim, the sublimity of the spirit, the kingdom of the Lord, and above all, the incomparable majesty of Almighty God—though I am acquainted with these things, yet am I not therefore by any means perfect; nor am I such a disciple as Paul or Peter. For many things are yet wanting to me, that I may not fall short of God.

Chapter VI.—Abstain from the poison of heretics.

I therefore, yet not I, but the love of Jesus Christ, entreat you that ye use Christian nourishment only, and abstain from herbage of a different kind; I mean heresy. For those [that are given to this] mix up Jesus Christ with their own poison, speaking things which are unworthy of credit, like those who administer a deadly drug in sweet wine, which he who is ignorant of does greedily take, with a fatal pleasure leading to his own death.
I therefore, yet not I, out the love of Jesus Christ, "entreat you that ye all speak the same thing, and that there be no divisions among you; but that ye be perfectly joined together in the same mind, and in the same judgment." For there are some vain talkers and deceivers, not Christians, but Christ-betrayers, bearing about the name of Christ in deceit, and "corrupting the word" of the Gospel; while they intermix the poison of their deceit with their persuasive talk, as if they mingled aconite with

sweet wine, that so he who drinks, being deceived in his taste by the very great sweetness of the draught, may incautiously meet with his death. One of the ancients gives us this advice, "Let no man be called good who mixes good with evil." For they speak of Christ, not that they may preach Christ, but that they may reject Christ; and they speak of the law, not that they may establish the law, but that they may proclaim things contrary to it. For they alienate Christ from the Father, and the law from Christ. They also calumniate His being born of the Virgin; they are ashamed of His cross; they deny His passion; and they do not believe His resurrection. They introduce God as a Being unknown; they suppose Christ to be unbegotten; and as to the Spirit, they do not admit that He exists. Some of them say that the Son is a mere man, and that the Father, Son, and Holy Spirit are but the same person, and that the creation is the work of God, not by Christ, but by some other strange power.

Chapter VII.—The same continued.

Be on your guard, therefore, against such persons. And this will be the case with you if you are not puffed up, and continue in intimate union with Jesus Christ our God, and the bishop, and the enactments of the apostles. He that is within the altar is pure, but he that is without is not pure; that is, he who does anything apart from the bishop, and presbytery, and deacons, such a man is not pure in his conscience.

Be on your guard, therefore, against such persons, that ye admit not of a snare for your own souls. And act so that your life shall be without offence to all men, lest ye become as "a snare upon a watch-tower, and as a net which is spread out." For "he that does not heal himself in his own works, is the brother of him that destroys himself." If, therefore, ye also put away conceit, arrogance, disdain, and haughtiness, it will be your privilege to be inseparably united to God, for "He is nigh unto those that fear Him." And says He, "Upon whom will I look, but upon him that is humble and quiet, and that trembles at my words?" And do ye also reverence your bishop as Christ Himself, according as the blessed apostles have enjoined you. He that is within the altar is pure, wherefore also he is obedient to the bishop and presbyters: but he that is without is one that does anything apart from the bishop, the presbyters, and the deacons. Such a person is defiled in his conscience, and is worse than an infidel. For what is the bishop but one who beyond all others possesses all power and authority, so far as it is possible for a man to possess it, who according to his ability has been made an imitator of the Christ of God? And what is the presbytery but a sacred assembly, the counsellors and assessors of the bishop? And what are the deacons but imitators of the angelic powers, fulfilling a pure and blameless ministry unto him, as the holy Stephen did to the blessed James, Timothy and Linus to Paul, Anencletus and Clement to Peter? He, therefore, that will not yield obedience to such, must needs be one utterly without God, an impious man who despises Christ, and depreciates His appointments.

Chapter VIII.—Be on your guard against the snares of the devil.

Not that I know there is anything of this kind among you; but I put you on your guard, inasmuch as I love you greatly, and foresee the snares of the devil. Wherefore, clothing yourselves with meekness, be ye renewed in faith, that is the flesh of the Lord, and in love, that is the blood of Jesus Christ. Let no one of you cherish any grudge against his neighbor. Give no occasion to the Gentiles, lest by means of a few foolish men the whole multitude [of those that believe] in God be evil spoken of. For, "Woe to him by whose vanity my name is blasphemed among any." Now I write these things unto you, not that I know there are any such persons among you; nay, indeed I hope that God will never permit any such report to reach my ears, He "who spared not His Son for the sake of His holy Church." But foreseeing the snares of the wicked one, I arm you beforehand by my admonitions, as my beloved and faithful children in Christ, furnishing you with the means of protection against the deadly disease of unruly men, by which do ye flee from the disease [referred to] by the good-will of Christ our Lord. Do ye therefore, clothing yourselves with meekness, become the imitators of His sufferings, and of His love, wherewith He loved us when He gave Himself a ransom for us, that He might cleanse us by His blood from our old ungodliness, and bestow life on us when we were almost on the point of perishing through the depravity that was in us. Let no one of you, therefore, cherish any grudge against his neighbor. For says our Lord, "Forgive, and it shall be forgiven unto you." Give no occasion to the Gentiles, lest "by means of a few foolish men the word and doctrine [of Christ] be blasphemed." For says the prophet, as in the person of God, "Woe to him by whom my name is blasphemed among the Gentiles."

Chapter IX.—Reference to the history of Christ.

Stop your ears, therefore, when any one speaks to you at variance with Jesus Christ, who was descended from David, and was also of Mary; who was truly born, and did eat and drink. He was truly persecuted under Pontius Pilate; He was truly crucified, and [truly] died, in the sight of beings in heaven, and on earth, and under the earth. He was also truly raised from the dead, His Father quickening Him, even as after the same manner His Father will so raise up us who believe in Him by Christ Jesus, apart from whom we do not possess the true life.

Stop your ears, therefore, when any one speaks to you at variance with Jesus Christ, the Son of God, who was descended from David, and was also of Mary; who was truly begotten of God and of the Virgin, but not after the same manner. For indeed God and man are not the same. He truly assumed a body; for "the Word was made flesh," and lived upon earth without sin. For says He, "Which of you convicted me of sin?" He did in reality both eat and drink. He was crucified and died under Pontius Pilate. He really, and not merely in appearance, was crucified, and died, in the sight of beings in heaven, and on earth, and under the earth. By those in heaven I mean such as are possessed of incorporeal natures; by those on earth, the Jews and Romans, and such persons as were present at that time when the Lord was crucified; and by those under the earth, the multitude that arose along with the Lord. For says the Scripture, "Many bodies of the saints that slept arose," their graves being opened. He descended, indeed, into Hades alone, but He arose accompanied by a multitude; and rent asunder that means of separation which had existed from the beginning of the world, and cast down its partition-wall. He also rose again in three days, the Father raising Him up; and after spending forty days with the apostles, He was received up to the Father, and "sat down at His right hand, expecting till His enemies are placed under His feet." On the day of the preparation, then, at the third hour, He received the sentence from Pilate, the Father permitting that to happen; at the sixth hour He was crucified; at the ninth hour He gave up the ghost; and before sunset He was buried. During the Sabbath He continued under the earth in the tomb in which Joseph of Arimathæa had laid Him. At the dawning of the Lord's Day He arose from the dead, according to what was spoken by Himself, "As Jonah was three days and three nights in the whale's belly, so shall the Son of man also be three days and three nights in the heart of the earth." The day of the preparation, then, comprises the passion; the Sabbath embraces the burial; the Lord's Day contains the resurrection.

Chapter X.—The reality of Christ's passion.

But if, as some that are without God, that is, the unbelieving, say, that He only seemed to suffer (they themselves only seeming to exist), then why am I in bonds? Why do I long to be exposed to the wild beasts? Do I therefore die in vain? Am I not then guilty of falsehood against [the cross of] the Lord?

But if, as some that are without God, that is, the unbelieving, say, He became man in appearance [only], that He did not in reality take unto Him a body, that He died in appearance [merely], and did not in very deed suffer, then for what reason am I now in bonds, and long to be exposed to the wild beasts? In such a case, I die in vain, and am guilty of falsehood against the cross of the Lord. Then also does the prophet in vain declare, "They shall look on Him whom they have pierced, and mourn over themselves as over one beloved." These men, therefore, are not less unbelievers than were those that crucified Him. But as for me, I do not place my hopes in one who died for me in appearance, but in reality. For that which is false is quite abhorrent to the truth. Mary then did truly conceive a body which had God inhabiting it. And God the Word was truly born of the Virgin, having clothed Himself with a body of like passions with our own. He who forms all men in the womb, was Himself really in the womb, and made for Himself a body of the seed of the Virgin, but without any intercourse of man. He was carried in the womb, even as we are, for the usual period of time; and was really born, as we also are; and was in reality nourished with milk, and partook of common meat and drink, even as we do. And when He had lived among men for thirty years, He was baptized by John, really and not in appearance; and when He had preached the Gospel three years, and done signs and wonders, He who was Himself the Judge was judged by the Jews, falsely so called, and by Pilate the governor; was scourged, was smitten on the cheek, was spit upon; He wore a crown of thorns and a purple robe; He was condemned: He was crucified in reality, and not in appearance, not in imagination, not in deceit. He really died, and was buried, and rose from the dead, even as He prayed in a certain place, saying, "But do Thou, O Lord, raise me up again, and I shall recompense them." And the Father, who always hears Him, answered and said, "Arise, O God, and judge the earth; for Thou shall receive all the heathen for Thine inheritance." The Father, therefore, who raised Him up, will also raise us up through Him, apart from whom no one will attain to true life. For says He, "I am the life; he that believeth in me, even though he die, shall live: and every one that lives and believeth in me, even though he die, shall live forever." Do ye therefore flee from these ungodly heresies; for they are the inventions of the devil, that serpent who was the author of evil, and who by means of the woman deceived Adam, the father of our race.

Chapter XI.—Avoid the deadly errors of the Docetæ.

Flee, therefore, those evil offshoots [of Satan], which produce death-bearing fruit, whereof if anyone tastes, he instantly dies. For these men are not the planting of the Father. For if they were, they would appear as branches of the cross, and their fruit would be incorruptible. By it He calls you through His passion, as being His members. The head, therefore, cannot be born by itself, without its members; God, who is [the Savior] Himself, having promised their union.

Do ye also avoid those wicked offshoots of his, Simon his firstborn son, and Menander, and Basilides, and all his wicked mob of followers, the worshippers of a man, whom also the prophet Jeremiah pronounces accursed. Flee also the impure Nicolaitanes, falsely so called, who are lovers of pleasure, and given to calumnious speeches. Avoid also the children of the evil one, Theodotus and Cleobulus, who produce death-bearing fruit, whereof if anyone tastes, he instantly dies, and that not a mere temporary death, but one that shall endure forever. These men are not the planting of the

Father, but are an accursed brood. And says the Lord, "Let every plant which my heavenly Father has not planted be rooted up." For if they had been branches of the Father, they would not have been "enemies of the cross of Christ," but rather of those who "killed the Lord of glory." But now, by denying the cross, and being ashamed of the passion, they cover the transgression of the Jews, those fighters against God, those murderers of the Lord; for it were too little to style them merely murderers of the prophets. But Christ invites you to [share in] His immortality, by His passion and resurrection, inasmuch as ye are His members.

Chapter XII.—Continue in unity and love.

I salute you from Smyrna, together with the Churches of God which are with me, who have refreshed me in all things, both in the flesh and in the spirit. My bonds, which I carry about with me for the sake of Jesus Christ (praying that I may attain to God), exhort you. Continue in harmony among yourselves, and in prayer with one another; for it becomes every one of you, and especially the presbyters, to refresh the bishop, to the honor of the Father, of Jesus Christ, and of the apostles. I entreat you in love to hear me, that I may not, by having written, be a testimony against you. And do ye also pray for me, who have need of your love, along with the mercy of God, that I may be worthy of the lot for which I am destined, and that I may not be found reprobate.

I salute you from Smyrna, together with the Churches of God which are with me, whose rulers have refreshed me in every respect, both in the flesh and in the spirit. My bonds, which I carry about with me for the sake of Jesus Christ (praying that I may attain to God), exhort you. Continue in harmony among yourselves, and in supplication; for it becomes every one of you, and especially the presbyters, to refresh the bishop, to the honor of the Father, and to the honor of Jesus Christ and of the apostles. I entreat you in love to hear me, that I may not, by having thus written, be a testimony against you. And do ye also pray for me, who have need of your love, along with the mercy of God, that I may be thought worthy to attain the lot for which I am now designed, and that I may not be found reprobate.

Chapter XIII.—Conclusion.

The love of the Smyrnæans and Ephesians salutes you. Remember in your prayers the Church which is in Syria, from which also I am not worthy to receive my appellation, being the last of them. Fare ye well in Jesus Christ, while ye continue subject to the bishop, as to the command [of God], and in like manner to the presbytery. And do ye, every man, love one another with an undivided heart. Let my spirit be sanctified by yours, not only now, but also when I shall attain to God. For I am as yet exposed to danger. But the Father is faithful in Jesus Christ to fulfil both mine and your petitions: in whom may ye be found unblameable.

The love of the Smyrnæans and Ephesians salutes you. Remember our Church which is in Syria, from which I am not worthy to receive my appellation, being the last of those of that place. Fare ye well in the Lord Jesus Christ, while ye continue subject to the bishop, and in like manner to the presbyters and to the deacons. And do ye, every man, love one another with an undivided heart. My spirit salutes you, not only now, but also when I shall have attained to God; for I am as yet exposed to danger. But the Father of Jesus Christ is faithful to fulfil both mine and your petitions: in whom may we be found without spot. May I have joy of you in the Lord.

The Epistle of Ignatius to the Romans Shorter and Longer Versions

Ignatius, who is also called Theophorus, to the Church which has obtained mercy, through the majesty of the Most High Father, and Jesus Christ, His only-begotten Son; the Church which is beloved and enlightened by the will of Him that willed all things which are according to the love of Jesus Christ our God, which also presides in the place of the region of the Romans, worthy of God, worthy of honor, worthy of the highest happiness, worthy of praise, worthy of obtaining her every desire, worthy of being deemed holy, and which presides over love, is named from Christ, and from the Father, which I also salute in the name of Jesus Christ, the Son of the Father: to those who are united, both according to the flesh and spirit, to every one of His commandments; who are filled inseparably with the grace of God, and are purified from every strange taint, [I wish] abundance of happiness unblameably, in Jesus Christ our God.

Ignatius, who is also called Theophorus, to the Church which has obtained mercy, through the majesty of the Most High God the Father, and of Jesus Christ, His only-begotten Son; the Church which is sanctified and enlightened by the will of God, who formed all things that are according to the faith and love of Jesus Christ, our God and Savior; the Church which presides in the place of the region of the Romans, and which is worthy of God, worthy of honor, worthy of the highest happiness, worthy of praise, worthy of credit, worthy of being deemed holy, and which presides over love, is named from Christ, and from the Father, and is possessed of the Spirit, which I also salute in the name of Almighty God, and of Jesus Christ His Son: to those who are united, both according to the flesh and spirit, to every one of His commandments, who are filled inseparably with all the grace of God, and are purified from every strange taint, [I wish] abundance of happiness unblameably, in God, even the Father, and our Lord Jesus Christ.

Chapter I.—As a prisoner, I hope to see you.

Through prayer to God I have obtained the privilege of seeing your most worthy faces, and have even been granted more than I requested; for I hope as a prisoner in Christ Jesus to salute you, if indeed it be the will of God that I be thought worthy of attaining unto the end. For the beginning has been well ordered, if I may obtain grace to cling to my lot without hindrance unto the end. For I am afraid of your love, lest it should do me an injury. For it is easy for you to accomplish what you please; but it is difficult for me to attain to God, if ye spare me.

Through prayer to God I have obtained the privilege of seeing your most worthy faces, even as I earnestly begged might be granted me; for as a prisoner in Christ Jesus I hope to salute you, if indeed it be the will [of God] that I be thought worthy of attaining unto the end. For the beginning has been well ordered, if I may obtain grace to cling to my lot without hindrance unto the end. For I am afraid of your love, lest it should do me an injury. For it is easy for you to accomplish what you please; but it is difficult for me to attain to God, if ye do not spare me, under the presence of carnal affection.

Chapter II.—Do not save me from martyrdom.

For it is not my desire to act towards you as a man-pleaser, but as pleasing God, even as also ye please Him. For neither shall I ever have such [another] opportunity of attaining to God; nor will ye, if ye shall now be silent, ever be entitled to the honor of a better work. For if ye are silent concerning me, I shall become God's; but if you show your love to my flesh, I shall again have to run my race. Pray, then, do not seek to confer any greater favor upon me than that I be sacrificed to God while the altar is still prepared; that, being gathered together in love, ye may sing praise to the Father, through Christ Jesus, that God has deemed me, the bishop of Syria, worthy to be sent for from the east unto the west. It is good to set from the world unto God, that I may rise again to Him.

For it is not my desire that ye should please men, but God, even as also ye do please Him. For neither shall I ever hereafter have such an opportunity of attaining to God; nor will ye, if ye shall now be silent, ever be entitled to the honor of a better work. For if ye are silent concerning me, I shall become God's; but if ye show your love to my flesh, I shall again have to run my race. Pray, then, do not seek to confer any greater favor upon me than that I be sacrificed to God, while the altar is still prepared; that, being gathered together in love, ye may sing praise to the Father, through Christ Jesus, that God has deemed me, the bishop of Syria, worthy to be sent for from the east unto the west, and to become a martyr in behalf of His own precious sufferings, so as to pass from the world to God, that I may rise again unto Him.

Chapter III.—Pray rather that I may attain to martyrdom.

Ye have never envied any one; ye have taught others. Now I desire that those things may be confirmed [by your conduct], which in your instructions ye enjoin [on others]. Only request in my behalf both inward and outward strength, that I may not only speak, but [truly] will; and that I may not merely be called a Christian, but really be found to be one. For if I be truly found [a Christian], I may also be called one, and be then deemed faithful, when I shall no longer appear to the world. Nothing visible is eternal. "For the things which are seen are temporal, but the things which are not seen are eternal." For our God, Jesus Christ, now that He is with the Father, is all the more revealed [in His glory]. Christianity is not a thing of silence only, but also of [manifest] greatness.

Ye have never envied any one; ye have taught others. Now I desire that those things may be confirmed [by your conduct], which in your instructions ye enjoin [on others]. Only request in my behalf both inward and outward strength, that I may not only speak, but [truly] will, so that I may not merely be called a Christian, but really found to be one. For if I be truly found [a Christian], I may also be called one, and be then deemed faithful, when I shall no longer appear to the world. Nothing visible is eternal. "For the things which are seen are temporal, but the things which are not seen are eternal." The Christian is not the result of persuasion, but of power. When he is hated by the world, he is beloved of God. For says [the Scripture], "If ye were of this world, the world would love its own; but now ye are not of the world, but I have chosen you out of it: continue in fellowship with me."

Chapter IV.—Allow me to fall a prey to the wild beasts.

I write to the Churches, and impress on them all, that I shall willingly die for God, unless ye hinder me. I beseech of you not to show an unseasonable good-will towards me. Suffer me to become food for the wild beasts, through whose instrumentality it will be granted me to attain to God. I am the wheat of God, and let me be ground by the teeth of the wild beasts, that I may be found the pure bread of Christ. Rather entice the wild beasts, that they may become my tomb, and may leave nothing of my body; so that when I have fallen asleep [in death], I may be no trouble to anyone. Then shall I truly be a disciple of Christ, when the world shall not see so much as my body. Entreat Christ for me, that by these instruments I may be found a sacrifice [to God]. I do not, as Peter and Paul, issue commandments unto you. They were apostles; I am but a condemned man: they were free, while I am, even until now, a servant. But when I suffer, I shall be the freed-man of Jesus, and shall rise again emancipated in Him. And now, being a prisoner, I learn not to desire anything worldly or vain.

I write to all the Churches, and impress on them all, that I shall willingly die for God, unless ye hinder me.

I beseech of you not to show an unseasonable good-will towards me. Suffer me to become food for the wild beasts, through whose instrumentality it will be granted me to attain to God. I am the wheat of God, and am ground by the teeth of the wild beasts, that I may be found the pure bread of God. Rather entice the wild beasts, that they may become my tomb, and may leave nothing of my body; so that when I have fallen asleep [in death], I may not be found troublesome to anyone. Then shall I be a true disciple of Jesus Christ, when the world shall not see so much as my body. Entreat the Lord for me, that by these instruments I may be found a sacrifice to God. I do not, as Peter and Paul, issue commandments unto you. They were apostles of Jesus Christ, but I am the very least [of believers]: they were free, as the servants of God; while I am, even until now, a servant. But when I suffer, I shall be the freed-man of Jesus Christ, and shall rise again emancipated in Him. And now, being in bonds for Him, I learn not to desire anything worldly or vain.

Chapter V.—I desire to die.

From Syria even unto Rome I fight with beasts, both by land and sea, both by night and day, being bound to ten leopards, I mean a band of soldiers, who, even when they receive benefits, show themselves all the worse. But I am the more instructed by their injuries [to act as a disciple of Christ]; "yet am I not thereby justified." May I enjoy the wild beasts that are prepared for me; and I pray they may be found eager to rush upon me, which also I will entice to devour me speedily, and not deal with me as with some, whom, out of fear, they have not touched. But if they be unwilling to assail me, I will compel them to do so. Pardon me [in this]: I know what is for my benefit. Now I begin to be a disciple. And let no one, of things visible or invisible, envy me that I should attain to Jesus Christ. Let fire and the cross; let the crowds of wild beasts; let tearings, breakings, and dislocations of bones; let cutting off of members; let shatterings of the whole body; and let all the dreadful torments of the devil come upon me: only let me attain to Jesus Christ.

From Syria even unto Rome I fight with beasts, both by land and sea, both by night and day, being bound to ten leopards, I mean a band of soldiers, who, even when they receive benefits, show themselves all the worse. But I am the more instructed by their injuries [to act as a disciple of Christ]; "yet am I not thereby justified." May I enjoy the wild beasts that are prepared for me; and I pray that they may be found eager to rush upon me, which also I will entice to devour me speedily, and not deal with me as with some, whom, out of fear, they have not touched. But if they be unwilling to assail me, I will compel them to do so. Pardon me [in this] I know what is for my benefit. Now I begin to be a disciple, and have no desire after anything visible or invisible, that I may attain to Jesus Christ. Let fire and the cross; let the crowds of wild beasts; let breakings, tearings, and separations of bones; let cutting off of members; let bruising to pieces of the whole body; and let the very torment of the devil come upon me: only let me attain to Jesus Christ.

Chapter VI.—By death I shall attain true life.

All the pleasures of the world, and all the kingdoms of this earth, shall profit me nothing. It is better for me to die in behalf of Jesus Christ, than to reign over all the ends of the earth. "For what shall a man be profited, if he gain the whole world, but lose his own soul?" Him I seek, who died for us: Him I desire, who rose again for our sake. This is the gain which is laid up for me. Pardon me, brethren: do not hinder me from living, do not wish to keep me in a state of death; and while I desire to belong to God, do not ye give me over to the world. Suffer me to obtain pure light: when I have gone thither, I shall indeed be a man of God. Permit me to be an imitator of the passion of my God. If anyone has Him within himself, let him consider what I desire, and let him have sympathy with me, as knowing how I am straitened.

All the ends of the world, and all the kingdoms of this earth, shall profit me nothing. It is better for me to die for the sake of Jesus Christ, than to reign over all the ends of the earth. "For what is a man profited, if he gain the whole world, but lose his own soul?" I long after the Lord, the Son of the true God and Father, even Jesus Christ. Him I seek, who died for us and rose again. Pardon me, brethren: do not hinder me in attaining to life; for Jesus is the life of believers. Do not wish to keep me in a state of death, for life without Christ is death. While I desire to belong to God, do not ye give me over to the world. Suffer me to obtain pure light: when I have gone thither, I shall indeed be a man of God. Permit me to be an imitator of the passion of Christ, my God. If anyone has Him within himself, let him consider what I desire, and let him have sympathy with me, as knowing how I am straitened.

Chapter VII.—Reason of desiring to die.

The prince of this world would fain carry me away, and corrupt my disposition towards God. Let none of you, therefore, who are [in Rome] help him; rather be ye on my side, that is, on the side of God. Do not speak of Jesus Christ, and yet set your desires on the world. Let not envy find a dwelling-place among you; nor even should I, when present with you, exhort you to it, be ye persuaded to listen to me, but rather give credit to those things which I now write to you. For though I am alive while I write to you, yet I am eager to die. My love has been crucified, and there is no fire in me desiring to be fed; but there is within me a water that lives and speaketh, saying to me inwardly, Come to the Father. I have no delight in corruptible food, nor in the pleasures of this life. I desire the bread of God, the heavenly bread, the bread of life, which is the flesh of Jesus Christ, the Son of God, who became afterwards of the seed of David and Abraham; and I desire the drink of God, namely His blood, which is incorruptible love and eternal life.

The prince of this world would fain carry me away, and corrupt my disposition towards God. Let none of you, therefore, who are [in Rome] help him; rather be ye on my side, that is, on the side of God. Do not speak of Jesus Christ, and yet prefer this world to Him. Let not envy find a dwelling-place among you; nor even should I, when present with you, exhort you to it, be ye persuaded, but rather give credit to those things which I now write to you. For though I am alive while I write to you, yet I am eager to die for the sake of Christ. My love has been crucified, and there is no fire in me that loves anything; but there is living water springing up in me, and which says to me inwardly, Come to the Father. I have no delight in corruptible food, nor in the pleasures of this life. I desire the bread of God, the heavenly bread, the bread of life, which is the flesh of Jesus Christ, the Son of God, who became afterwards of the seed of David and Abraham; and I desire the drink, namely His blood, which is incorruptible love and eternal life.

Chapter VIII.—Be ye favorable to me.

I no longer wish to live after the manner of men, and my desire shall be fulfilled if ye consent. Be ye willing, then, that ye also may have your desires fulfilled. I entreat you in this brief letter; do ye give credit to me. Jesus Christ will reveal these things to you, [so that ye shall know] that I speak truly. He is the mouth altogether free from falsehood, by which the Father has truly spoken. Pray you for me, that I may attain [the object of my desire]. I have not written to you according to the flesh, but according to the will of God. If I shall suffer, ye have wished [well] to me; but if I am rejected, ye have hated me.

I no longer wish to live after the manner of men, and my desire shall be fulfilled if ye consent. "I am crucified with Christ: nevertheless I live; yet no longer I, since Christ lives in me." I entreat you in this brief letter: do not refuse me; believe me that I love Jesus, who was delivered [to death] for my sake. "What shall I render to the Lord for all His benefits towards me?" Now God, even the Father, and the Lord Jesus Christ, shall reveal these things to you, [so that ye shall know] that I speak truly. And do ye pray along with me, that I may attain my aim in the Holy Spirit. I have not written to you according to the flesh, but according to the will of God. If I shall suffer, ye have loved me; but if I am rejected, ye have hated me.

Chapter IX.—Pray for the church in Syria.

Remember in your prayers the Church in Syria, which now has God for its shepherd, instead of me. Jesus Christ alone will oversee it, and your love [will also regard it]. But as for me, I am ashamed to be counted one of them; for indeed I am not worthy, as being the very last of them, and one born out of due time. But I have obtained mercy to be somebody, if I shall attain to God. My spirit salutes you, and the love of the Churches that have received me in the name of Jesus Christ, and not as a mere passer-by. For even those Churches which were not near to me in the way, I mean according to the flesh, have gone before me, city by city, [to meet me.]

Remember in your prayers the Church which is in Syria, which, instead of me, has now for its shepherd the Lord, who says, "I am the good Shepherd." And He alone will oversee it, as well as your love towards Him. But as for me, I am ashamed to be counted one of them; for I am not worthy, as being the very last of them, and one born out of due time. But I have obtained mercy to be somebody, if I shall attain to God. My spirit salutes you, and the love of the Churches which have received me in the name of Jesus Christ, and not as a mere passer-by. For even those Churches which were not near to me in the way, have brought me forward, city by city.

Chapter X.—Conclusion.

Now I write these things to you from Smyrna by the Ephesians, who are deservedly most happy. There is also with me, along with many others, Crocus, one dearly beloved by me. As to those who have gone before me from Syria to Rome for the glory of God, I believe that you are acquainted with them; to whom, [then,] do ye make known that I am at hand. For they are all worthy, both of God and of you; and it is becoming that you should refresh them in all things. I have written these things unto you, on the day before the ninth of the Kalends of September (that is, on the twenty-third day of August). Fare ye well to the end, in the patience of Jesus Christ. Amen.

The Epistle of Ignatius to the Philadelphians Shorter and Longer Versions

Ignatius, who is also called Theophorus, to the Church of God the Father, and our Lord Jesus Christ, which is at Philadelphia, in Asia, which has obtained mercy, and is established in the harmony of God, and rejoices unceasingly in the passion of our Lord, and is filled with all mercy through his resurrection; which I salute in the blood of Jesus Christ, who is our eternal and enduring joy, especially if [men] are in unity with the bishop, the presbyters, and the deacons, who have been appointed according to the mind of Jesus Christ, whom He has established in security, after His own will, and by His Holy Spirit.

Ignatius, who is also called Theophorus, to the Church of God the Father, and of the Lord Jesus Christ, which is at Philadelphia, which has obtained mercy through love, and is established in the harmony of God, and rejoices unceasingly, in the passion of our Lord Jesus, and is filled with all mercy through His resurrection; which I salute in the blood of Jesus Christ, who is our eternal and enduring joy, especially to those who are in unity with the bishop, and the presbyters, and the deacons, who have been appointed by the will of God the Father, through the Lord Jesus Christ, who, according to His own will, has firmly established His Church upon a rock, by a spiritual building, not made with hands, against which the winds and the floods have beaten, yet have not been able to overthrow it: yea, and may spiritual wickedness never be able to do so, but be thoroughly weakened by the power of Jesus Christ our Lord.

Chapter I.—Praise of the bishop.

Which bishop, I know, obtained the ministry which pertains to the common [weal], not of himself, neither by men, nor through vainglory, but by the love of God the Father, and the Lord Jesus Christ; at whose meekness I am struck with admiration, and who by his silence is able to accomplish more than those who vainly talk. For he is in harmony with the commandments [of God], even as the harp is with its strings. Wherefore my soul declares his mind towards God a happy one, knowing it to be virtuous and perfect, and that his stability as well as freedom from all anger is after the example of the infinite meekness of the living God.

Having beheld your bishop, I know that he was not selected to undertake the ministry which pertains to the common [weal], either by himself or by men, or out of vainglory, but by the love of Jesus Christ, and of God the Father, who raised Him from the dead; at whose meekness I am struck with admiration, and who by His silence is able to accomplish more than they who talk a great deal. For he is in harmony with the commandments and ordinances of the Lord, even as the strings are with the harp, and is no less blameless than was Zacharias the priest. Wherefore my soul declares his mind towards God a happy one, knowing it to be virtuous and perfect, and that his stability as well as freedom from all anger is after the example of the infinite meekness of the living God.

Chapter II.—Maintain union with the bishop.

Wherefore, as children of light and truth, flee from division and wicked doctrines; but where the shepherd is, there do ye as sheep follow. For there are many wolves that appear worthy of credit, who, by means of a pernicious pleasure, carry captive those that are running towards God; but in your unity they shall have no place.

Wherefore, as children of light and truth, avoid the dividing of your unity, and the wicked doctrine of the heretics, from whom "a defiling influence has gone forth into all the earth." But where the shepherd is, there do ye as sheep follow. For there are many wolves in sheep's clothing, who, by means of a pernicious pleasure, carry captive those that are running towards God; but in your unity they shall have no place.

Chapter III.—Avoid schismatics.

Keep yourselves from those evil plants which Jesus Christ does not tend, because they are not the planting of the Father. Not that I have found any division among you, but exceeding purity. For as many as are of God and of Jesus Christ are also with the bishop. And as many as shall, in the exercise of repentance, return into the unity of the Church, these, too, shall belong to God, that they may live according to Jesus Christ. Do not err, my brethren. If any man follows him that makes a schism in the Church, he shall not inherit the kingdom of God. If anyone walks according to a strange opinion, he agrees not with the passion [of Christ.].

Keep yourselves, then, from those evil plants which Jesus Christ does not tend, but that wild beast, the destroyer of men, because they are not the planting of the Father, but the seed of the wicked one. Not that I have found any division among you do I write these things; but I arm you beforehand, as the children of God. For as many as are of Christ are also with the bishop; but as many as fall away from him, and embrace communion with the accursed, these shall be cut off along with them. For they are not Christ's husbandry, but the seed of the enemy, from whom may you ever be delivered by the prayers of the shepherd, that most faithful and gentle shepherd who presides over you. I therefore exhort you in the Lord to receive with all tenderness those that repent and return to the unity of the Church, that through your kindness and forbearance they may recover themselves out of the snare of the devil, and becoming worthy of Jesus Christ, may obtain eternal salvation in the kingdom of Christ. Brethren, be not deceived. If any man follows him that separates from the truth, he shall not inherit the kingdom of God; and if any man does not stand aloof from the preacher of falsehood, he shall be condemned to hell. For it is obligatory neither to separate from the godly, nor to associate with the ungodly. If anyone walks according to a strange opinion, he is not of Christ, nor a partaker of His passion; but is a fox, a destroyer of the vineyard of Christ. Have no fellowship with such a man, lest ye perish along with him, even should he be thy father, thy son, thy brother, or a member of thy family. For says [the Scripture], "Thine eye shall not spare him." You ought therefore to "hate those that hate God, and to waste away [with grief] on account of His enemies." I do not mean that you should beat them or persecute them, as do the Gentiles "that know not the Lord and God;" but that you should regard them as your enemies, and separate yourselves from them, while yet you admonish them, and exhort them to repentance, if it may be they will hear, if it may be they will submit themselves. For our God is a lover of mankind, and "will have all men to be saved, and to come to the knowledge of the truth." Wherefore "He makes His sun to rise upon the evil and on the good, and sendeth rain on the just and on the unjust;" of whose kindness the Lord, wishing us also to be imitators, says, "Be ye perfect, even as also your Father that is in heaven is perfect."

Chapter IV.—Have but one Eucharist, etc.

Take ye heed, then, to have but one Eucharist. For there is one flesh of our Lord Jesus Christ, and one cup to [show forth] the unity of His blood; one altar; as there is one bishop, along with the presbytery and deacons, my fellow-servants: that so, whatsoever ye do, ye may do it according to [the will of] God.
I have confidence of you in the Lord, that ye will be of no other mind. Wherefore I write boldly to your

love, which is worthy of God, and exhort you to have but one faith, and one [kind of] preaching, and one Eucharist. For there is one flesh of the Lord Jesus Christ; and His blood which was shed for us is one; one loaf also is broken to all [the communicants], and one cup is distributed among them all: there is but one altar for the whole Church, and one bishop, with the presbytery and deacons, my fellow-servants. Since, also, there is but one unbegotten Being, God, even the Father; and one only-begotten Son, God, the Word and man; and one Comforter, the Spirit of truth; and also one preaching, and one faith, and one baptism; and one Church which the holy apostles established from one end of the earth to the other by the blood of Christ, and by their own sweat and toil; it behooves you also, therefore, as "a peculiar people, and a holy nation," to perform all things with harmony in Christ. Wives, be ye subject to your husbands in the fear of God; and ye virgins, to Christ in purity, not counting marriage an abomination, but desiring that which is better, not for the reproach of wedlock, but for the sake of meditating on the law. Children, obey your parents, and have an affection for them, as workers together with God for your birth [into the world]. Servants, be subject to your masters in God, that ye may be the freed-men of Christ. Husbands, love your wives, as fellow-servants of God, as your own body, as the partners of your life, and your co-adjutors in the procreation of children. Virgins, have Christ alone before your eyes, and His Father in your prayers, being enlightened by the Spirit. May I have pleasure in your purity, as that of Elijah, or as of Joshua the son of Nun, as of Melchizedek, or as of Elisha, as of Jeremiah, or as of John the Baptist, as of the beloved disciple, as of Timothy, as of Titus, as of Evodius, as of

Clement, who departed this life in [perfect] chastity, Not, however, that I blame the other blessed [saints] because they entered into the married state, of which I have just spoken. For I pray that, being found worthy of God, I may be found at their feet in the kingdom, as at the feet of Abraham, and Isaac, and Jacob; as of Joseph, and Isaiah, and the rest of the prophets; as of Peter, and Paul, and the rest of the apostles, that were married men. For they entered into these marriages not for the sake of appetite, but out of regard for the propagation of mankind. Fathers, "bring up your children in the nurture and admonition of the Lord;" and teach them the Holy Scriptures, and also trades, that they may not indulge in idleness. Now [the Scripture] says, "A righteous father educates [his children] well; his heart shall rejoice in a wise son." Masters, be gentle towards your servants, as holy Job has taught you; for there is one nature, and one family of mankind. For "in Christ there is neither bond nor free." Let governors be obedient to Cæsar; soldiers to those that command them; deacons to the presbyters, as to high-priests; the presbyters, and deacons, and the rest of the clergy, together with all the people, and the soldiers, and the governors, and Cæsar [himself], to the bishop; the bishop to Christ, even as Christ to the Father. And thus unity is preserved throughout. Let not the widows be wanderers about, nor fond of dainties, nor gadders from house to house; but let them be like Judith, noted for her seriousness; and like Anna, eminent for her sobriety. I do not ordain these things as an apostle: for "who am I, or what is my father's house," that I should pretend to be equal in honor to them? But as your "fellow-soldier," I hold the position of one who [simply] admonishes you.

Chapter V.—Pray for me.

My brethren, I am greatly enlarged in loving you; and rejoicing exceedingly [over you], I seek to secure your safety. Yet it is not I, but Jesus Christ, for whose sake being bound I fear the more, inasmuch as I am not yet perfect. But your prayer to God shall make me perfect, that I may attain to that portion which through mercy has been allotted me, while I flee to the Gospel as to the flesh of Jesus, and to the apostles as to the presbytery of the Church. And let us also love the prophets, because they too have proclaimed the Gospel, and placed their hope in Him, and waited for Him; in whom also believing, they were saved, through union to Jesus Christ, being holy men, worthy of love and admiration, having had witness borne to them by Jesus Christ, and being reckoned along with [us] in the Gospel of the common hope.

My brethren, I am greatly enlarged in loving you; and rejoicing exceedingly [over you], I seek to secure your safety. Yet it is not I, but the Lord Jesus through me; for whose sake being bound, I fear the more, for I am not yet perfect. But your prayer to God shall make me perfect, that I may attain that to which I have been called, while I flee to the Gospel as to the flesh of Jesus Christ, and to the apostles as the presbytery of the Church. I do also love the prophets as those who announced Christ, and as being partakers of the same Spirit with the apostles. For as the false prophets and the false apostles drew [to themselves] one and the same wicked, deceitful, and seducing438 spirit; so also did the prophets and the apostles receive from God, through Jesus Christ, one and the same Holy Spirit, who is good, and sovereign, and true, and the Author of [saving] knowledge. For there is one God of the

Old and New Testament, "one Mediator between God and men," for the creation of both intelligent and sensitive beings, and in order to exercise a beneficial and suitable providence [over them]. There is also one Comforter, who displayed His power in Moses, and the prophets, and apostles. All the saints, therefore, were saved by Christ, hoping in Him, and waiting for Him; and they obtained through Him salvation, being holy ones, worthy of love and admiration, having testimony borne to them by Jesus Christ, in the Gospel of our common hope.

Chapter VI.—Do not accept Judaism.

But if anyone preach the Jewish law unto you, listen not to him. For it is better to hearken to Christian doctrine from a man who has been circumcised, than to Judaism from one uncircumcised. But if either of such persons do not speak concerning Jesus Christ, they are in my judgment but as monuments and sepulchers of the dead, upon which are written only the names of men. Flee therefore the wicked devices and snares of the prince of this world, lest at any time being conquered by his artifices, ye grow weak in your love. But be ye all joined together with an undivided heart. And I thank my God that I have a good conscience in respect to you, and that no one has it in his power to boast, either privately or publicly, that I have burdened any one either in much or in little. And I wish for all among whom I have spoken, that they may not possess that for a testimony against them.

If anyone preaches the one God of the law and the prophets, but denies Christ to be the Son of God, he is a liar, even as also is his father the devil, and is a Jew falsely so called, being possessed of mere carnal circumcision. If anyone confesses Christ Jesus the Lord, but denies the God of the law and of the prophets, saying that the Father of Christ is not the Maker of heaven and earth, he has not continued in the truth any more than his father the devil, and is a disciple of Simon Magus, not of the Holy Spirit. If anyone says there is one God, and also confesses Christ Jesus, but thinks the Lord to be a mere man, and not the only-begotten God, and Wisdom, and the Word of God, and deems Him to consist merely of a soul and body, such an one is a serpent, that preaches deceit and error for the destruction of men. And such a man is poor in understanding, even as by name he is an Ebionite. If anyone confesses the truths mentioned, but calls lawful wedlock, and the procreation of children, destruction and pollution, or deems certain kinds of food abominable, such a one has the apostate dragon dwelling within him. If anyone confesses the Father, and the Son, and the Holy Ghost, and praises the creation, but calls the incarnation merely an appearance, and is ashamed of the passion, such a one has denied the faith, not less than the Jews who killed Christ. If anyone confesses these things, and that God the Word did dwell in a human body, being within it as the Word, even as the soul also is in the body, because it was God that inhabited it, and not a human soul, but affirms that unlawful unions are a good thing, and places the highest happiness in pleasure, as does the man who is falsely called a Nicolaitan, this person can neither be a lover of God, nor a lover of Christ, but is a corrupter of his own flesh, and therefore void of the Holy Spirit, and a stranger to Christ. All such persons are but monuments and sepulchers of the dead, upon which are written only the names of dead men. Flee, therefore, the wicked devices and snares of the spirit which now worketh in the children of this world, lest at any time being overcome, ye grow weak in your love. But be ye all joined together with an undivided heart and a willing mind, "being of one accord and of one judgment," being always of the same opinion about the same things, both when you are at ease and in danger, both in sorrow and in joy. I thank God, through Jesus Christ, that I have a good conscience in respect to you, and that no one has it in his power to boast, either privately or publicly, that I have burdened any one either in much or in little. And I wish for all among whom I have spoken, that they may not possess that for a testimony against them.

Chapter VII.—I have exhorted you to unity.

For though some would have deceived me according to the flesh, yet the Spirit, as being from God, is not deceived. For it knows both whence it comes and whither it goes, and detects the secrets [of the heart]. For, when I was among you, I cried, I spoke with a loud voice: Give heed to the bishop, and to the presbytery and deacons. Now, some suspected me of having spoken thus, as knowing beforehand the division caused by some among you. But He is my witness, for whose sake I am in bonds, that I got no intelligence from any man. But the Spirit proclaimed these words: Do nothing without the bishop; keep your bodies as the temples of God; love unity; avoid divisions; be the followers of Jesus Christ, even as He is of His Father.

For though some would have deceived me according to the flesh, yet my spirit is not deceived; for I have received it from God. For it knows both whence it comes and whither it goes, and detects the secrets [of the heart]. For when I was among you, I cried, I spoke with a loud voice—the word is not mine, but God's—Give heed to the bishop, and to the presbytery and deacons. But if ye suspect that I spoke thus, as having learned beforehand the division caused by some among you, He is my witness, for whose sake I am in bonds, that I learned nothing of it from the mouth of any man. But the Spirit made an announcement to me, saying as follows: Do nothing without the bishop; keep your bodies as the temples of God; love unity; avoid divisions; be ye followers of Paul, and of the rest of the apostles, even as they also were of Christ.

Chapter VIII.—The same continued.

I therefore did what belonged to me, as a man devoted to unity. For where there is division and wrath, God doth not dwell. To all them that repent, the Lord grants forgiveness, if they turn in penitence to the unity of God, and to communion with the bishop. I trust [as to you] in the grace of Jesus Christ, who shall free you from every bond. And I exhort you to do nothing out of strife, but according to the doctrine of Christ. When I heard some saying, If I do not find it in the ancient Scriptures, I will not believe the Gospel; on my saying to them, It is written, they answered me, That remains to be proved. But to me Jesus Christ is in the place of all that is ancient: His cross, and death, and resurrection, and the faith which is by Him, are undefiled monuments of antiquity; by which I desire, through your prayers, to be justified. I therefore did what belonged to me, as a man devoted to unity; adding this also, that where there is diversity of judgment, and wrath, and hatred, God does not dwell. To all them that repent, God grants forgiveness, if they with one consent return to the unity of Christ, and communion with the bishop. I trust to the grace of Jesus Christ, that He will free you from every bond of wickedness. I therefore exhort you that ye do nothing out of strife, but according to the doctrine of Christ. For I have heard some saying, If I do not find the Gospel in the archives, I will not believe it. To such persons I say that my archives are Jesus Christ, to disobey whom is manifest destruction. My authentic archives are His cross, and death, and resurrection, and the faith which bears on these things, by which I desire, through your prayers, to be justified. He who disbelieves the Gospel disbelieves everything along with it. For the archives ought not to be preferred to the Spirit. "It is hard to kick against the pricks;" it is hard to disbelieve Christ; it is hard to reject the preaching of the apostles.

Chapter IX.—The Old Testament is good: the New Testament is better.

The priests indeed are good, but the High Priest is better; to whom the holy of holies has been committed, and who alone has been trusted with the secrets of God. He is the door of the Father, by which enter in Abraham, and Isaac, and Jacob, and the prophets, and the apostles, and the Church. All these have for their object the attaining to the unity of God. But the Gospel possesses something transcendent [above the former dispensation], viz., the appearance of our Lord Jesus Christ, His passion and resurrection. For the beloved prophets announced Him, but the Gospel is the perfection of immortality. All these things are good together, if ye believe in love.

The priests indeed, and the ministers of the word, are good; but the High Priest is better, to whom the holy of holies has been committed, and who alone has been entrusted with the secrets of God. The ministering powers of God are good. The Comforter is holy, and the Word is holy, the Son of the Father, by whom He made all things, and exercises a providence over them all. This is the Way which leads to the Father, the Rock, the Defense, the Key, the Shepherd, the Sacrifice, the Door of knowledge, through which have entered Abraham, and Isaac, and Jacob, Moses and all the company of the prophets, and these pillars of the world, the apostles, and the spouse of Christ, on whose account He poured out His own blood, as her marriage portion, that He might redeem her. All these things tend towards the unity of the one and only true God. But the Gospel possesses something transcendent [above the former dispensation], viz. the appearing of our Savior Jesus Christ, His passion, and the resurrection itself. For those things which the prophets announced, saying, "Until He come for whom it is reserved, and He shall be the expectation of the Gentiles," have been fulfilled in the Gospel, [our Lord saying,] "Go ye and teach all nations, baptizing them in the name of the Father, and of the Son, and of the Holy Ghost." All then are good together, the law, the prophets, the apostles, the whole company [of others] that have believed through them: only if we love one another.

Chapter X.—Congratulate the inhabitants of Antioch on the close of the persecution.

Since, according to your prayers, and the

compassion which ye feel in Christ Jesus, it is reported to me that the Church which is at Antioch in Syria possesses peace, it will become you, as a Church of God, to elect a deacon to act as the ambassador of God [for you] to [the brethren there], that he may rejoice along with them when they are met together, and glorify the name [of God]. Blessed is he in Jesus Christ, who shall be deemed worthy of such a ministry; and ye too shall be glorified. And if ye are willing, it is not beyond your power to do this, for the sake of God; as also the nearest Churches have sent, in some cases bishops, and in others presbyters and deacons. Since, according to your prayers, and the compassion which ye feel in Christ Jesus, it is reported to me that the Church which is at Antioch in Syria possesses peace, it will become you, as a Church of God, to elect a bishop to act as the ambassador of God [for you] to [the brethren] there, that it may be granted them to meet together, and to glorify the name of God. Blessed is he in Christ Jesus, who shall be deemed worthy of such a ministry; and if ye be zealous [in this matter], ye shall receive glory in Christ. And if ye are willing, it is not altogether beyond your power to do this, for the sake of God; as also the nearest Churches have sent, in some cases bishops, and in others presbyters and deacons.

Chapter XI.—Thanks and salutation.

Now, as to Philo the deacon, of Cilicia, a man of reputation, who still ministers to me in the word of God, along with Rheus Agathopus, an elect man, who has followed me from Syria, not regarding his life,—these bear witness in your behalf; and I myself give thanks to God for you, that ye have received them, even as the Lord you. But may those that dishonored them be forgiven through the grace of Jesus Christ! The love of the brethren at Troas salutes you; whence also I write to you by Burrhus, who was sent along with me by the Ephesians and Smyrnæans, to show their respect. May the Lord Jesus Christ honor them, in whom they hope, in flesh, and soul, and faith, and love, and concord! Fare ye well in Christ Jesus, our common hope. Now, as to Philo the deacon, a man of Cilicia, of high reputation, who still ministers to me in the word of God, along with Gaius and Agathopus, an elect man, who has followed me from Syria, not regarding his life,—these also bear testimony in your behalf. And I myself give thanks to God for you, because ye have received them: and the Lord will also receive you. But may those that dishonored them be forgiven through the grace of Jesus Christ, "who wishes not the death of the sinner, but his repentance." The love of the brethren at Troas salutes you; whence also I write to you by Burrhus, who was sent along with me by the Ephesians and Smyrnæans, to show their respect: whom the Lord Jesus Christ will requite, in whom they hope, in flesh, and soul, and spirit, and faith, and love, and concord. Fare ye well in the Lord Jesus Christ, our common hope, in the Holy Ghost.

The Epistle of Ignatius to the Smyrnæans Shorter and Longer Versions.

Ignatius, who is also called Theophorus, to the Church of God the Father, and of the beloved Jesus Christ, which has through mercy obtained every kind of gift, which is filled with faith and love, and is deficient in no gift, most worthy of God, and adorned with holiness:

the Church which is at Smyrna, in Asia, wishes abundance of happiness, through the immaculate Spirit and word of God.

Ignatius, who is also called Theophorus, to the Church of God the most high Father, and His beloved Son Jesus Christ, which has through mercy obtained every kind of gift, which is filled with faith and love, and is deficient in no gift, most worthy of God, and adorned with holiness: the Church which is at Smyrna, in Asia, wishes abundance of happiness, through the immaculate Spirit and word of God.

Chapter I.—Thanks to God for your faith.

I Glorify God, even Jesus Christ, who has given you such wisdom. For I have observed that ye are perfected in an immoveable faith, as if ye were nailed to the cross of our Lord Jesus Christ, both in the flesh and in the spirit, and are established in love through the blood of Christ, being fully persuaded with respect to our Lord, that He was truly of the seed of David according to the flesh, and the Son of God according to the will and power of God; that He was truly born of a virgin, was baptized by John, in order that all righteousness might be fulfilled by Him; and was truly, under Pontius Pilate and Herod the tetrarch, nailed [to the cross] for us in His flesh. Of this fruit we are by His divinely-blessed passion, that He might set up a standard for all ages, through His resurrection, to all His holy and faithful [followers], whether among Jews or Gentiles, in the one body of His Church.

I Glorify the God and Father of our Lord Jesus Christ, who by Him has given you such wisdom. For I have observed that ye are perfected in an immoveable faith, as if ye were nailed to the cross of our Lord Jesus Christ, both in the flesh and in the spirit, and are established in love through the blood of Christ, being fully persuaded, in very truth, with respect to our Lord Jesus Christ, that He was the Son of God, "the first-born of every creature," God the Word, the only-begotten Son, and was of the seed of David according to the flesh, by the Virgin Mary; was baptized by John, that all righteousness might be fulfilled by Him; that He lived a life of holiness without sin, and was truly, under Pontius Pilate and Herod the tetrarch, nailed [to the cross] for us in His flesh. From whom we also derive our being, from His divinely-blessed passion, that He might set up a standard for the ages, through His resurrection, to all His holy and faithful [followers], whether among Jews or Gentiles, in the one body of His Church.

Chapter II.—Christ's true passion.

Now, He suffered all these things for our sakes, that we might be saved. And He suffered truly, even as also He truly raised up Himself, not, as certain unbelievers maintain, that He only seemed to suffer, as they themselves only seem to be [Christians]. And as they believe, so shall it happen unto them, when they shall be divested of their bodies, and be mere evil spirits.

Now, He suffered all these things for us; and He suffered them really, and not in appearance only, even as also He truly rose again. But not, as some of the unbelievers, who are ashamed of the formation of man, and the cross, and death itself, affirm, that in appearance only, and not in truth, He took a body of the Virgin, and suffered only in appearance, forgetting, as they do, Him who said, "The Word was made flesh;" and again, "Destroy this temple, and in three days I will raise it up;" and once more, "If I be lifted up from the earth, I will draw all men unto Me." The Word therefore did dwell in flesh, for "Wisdom built herself a house." The Word raised up again His own temple on the third day, when it had been destroyed by the Jews fighting against Christ. The Word, when His flesh was lifted up, after the manner of the brazen serpent in the wilderness, drew all men to Himself for their eternal salvation.

Chapter III.—Christ was possessed of a body after His resurrection.

For I know that after His resurrection also He was still possessed of flesh, and I believe that He is so now. When, for instance, He came to those who were with Peter, He said to them, "Lay hold, handle Me, and see that I am not an incorporeal spirit." And immediately they touched Him, and believed, being convinced both by His flesh and spirit. For this cause also they despised death, and were found its conquerors. And after his resurrection He did eat and drink with them, as being possessed of flesh, although spiritually He was united to the Father.

And I know that He was possessed of a body not only in His being born and crucified, but I also know that He was so after His resurrection, and believe that He is so now. When, for instance, He came to those who were with Peter, He said to them, "Lay hold, handle Me, and see that I am not an incorporeal spirit." "For a spirit hath not flesh and bones, as ye see Me have." And He says to Thomas, "Reach hither thy finger into the print of the nails, and reach hither thy hand, and thrust it into My side;" and immediately they believed that He was Christ. Wherefore Thomas also says to Him, "My Lord, and my God." And on this account also did they despise death, for it were too little to say, indignities and stripes. Nor was this all; but also after He had shown Himself to them, that He had risen indeed, and not in appearance only, He both ate and drank with them during forty entire days. And thus was He, with the flesh, received up in their sight unto Him that sent Him, being with that same flesh to come again, accompanied by glory and power. For, say the [holy] oracles, "This same Jesus, who is taken up from you into heaven, shall so come, in like manner as ye have seen Him go unto heaven." But if they say that He will come at the end of the world without a body, how shall those "see Him that pierced Him," and when they recognize Him, "mourn for themselves?" For incorporeal beings have neither form nor figure, nor the aspect of an animal possessed of shape, because their nature is in itself simple.

Chapter IV.—Beware of these heretics.

I give you these instructions, beloved, assured that ye also hold the same opinions [as I do]. But I guard you beforehand from those beasts in the shape of men, whom you must not only not receive, but, if it be possible, not even meet with; only you must pray to God for them, if by any means they may be brought to repentance, which, however, will be very difficult. Yet Jesus Christ, who is our true life, has the power of [effecting] this. But if these things were done by our Lord only in appearance, then am I also only in appearance bound. And why have I also surrendered myself to death, to fire, to the sword, to the wild beasts? But, [in fact,] he who is near to the sword is near to God; he that is among the wild beasts is in company with God; provided only he be so in the name of Jesus Christ. I undergo all these things that I may suffer together with Him, He who became a perfect man inwardly strengthening me.

I give you these instructions, beloved, assured that ye also hold the same opinions [as I do]. But I guard you beforehand from these beasts in the shape of men, from whom you must not only turn away, but even flee from them. Only you must pray for them, if by any means they may be brought to repentance. For if the Lord were in the body in appearance only, and were crucified in appearance only, then am I also bound in appearance only. And why have I also surrendered myself to death, to fire, to the sword, to the wild beasts? But, [in fact,] I endure all things for Christ, not in appearance only, but in reality, that I may suffer together with Him, while He Himself inwardly strengthens me; for of myself I have no such ability.

Chapter V.—Their dangerous errors.

Some ignorantly deny Him, or rather have been denied by Him, being the advocates of death rather than of the truth. These persons neither have the prophets persuaded, nor the law of Moses, nor the Gospel even to this day, nor the sufferings we have individually endured. For they think also the same thing regarding us. For what does anyone profit me, if he commends me, but blasphemes my Lord, not confessing that He was [truly] possessed of a body? But he who does not acknowledge this, has in fact altogether denied Him, being enveloped in death. I have not, however, thought good to write the names of such persons, inasmuch as they are unbelievers. Yea, far be it from me to make any mention of them, until they repent and return to [a true belief in] Christ's passion, which is our resurrection.

Some have ignorantly denied Him, and advocate falsehood rather than the truth. These persons neither have the prophecies persuaded, nor the Law of Moses, nor the Gospel even to this day, nor the sufferings we have individually endured. For they think also the same thing regarding us. For what does it profit, if any one commends me, but blasphemes my Lord, not owning Him to be God incarnate? He that does not confess this, has in fact altogether denied Him, being enveloped in death. I have not, however, thought good to write the names of such persons, inasmuch as they are unbelievers; and far be it from me to make any mention of them, until they repent.

Chapter VI—Unbelievers in the blood of Christ shall be condemned.

Let no man deceive himself. Both the things which are in heaven, and the glorious angels, and rulers, both visible and invisible, if they believe not in the blood of Christ, shall, in consequence, incur condemnation. "He that is able to receive it, let him receive it." Let not [high] place puff any one up: for that which is worth all is faith and love, to which nothing is to be preferred. But consider those who are of a different opinion with respect to the grace of Christ which has come unto us, how opposed they are to the will of God. They have no regard for love;

no care for the widow, or the orphan, or the oppressed; of the bond, or of the free; of the hungry, or of the thirsty.

Let no man deceive himself. Unless he believes that Christ Jesus has lived in the flesh, and shall confess His cross and passion, and the blood which He shed for the salvation of the world, he shall not obtain eternal life, whether he be a king, or a priest, or a ruler, or a private person, a master or a servant, a man or a woman. "He that is able to receive it, let him receive it." Let no man's place, or dignity, or riches, puff him up; and let no man's low condition or poverty abase him. For the chief points are faith towards God, hope towards Christ, the enjoyment of those good things for which we look, and love towards God and our neighbor. For, "Thou shall love the Lord thy God with all thy heart, and thy neighbor as thyself." And the Lord says, "This is life eternal, to know the only true God, and Jesus Christ whom He has sent." And again, "A new commandment give I unto you, that ye love one another. On these two commandments hang all the law and the prophets." Do ye, therefore, notice those who preach other doctrines, how they affirm that the Father of Christ cannot be known, and how they exhibit enmity and deceit in their dealings with one another. They have no regard for love; they despise the good things we expect hereafter; they regard present things as if they were durable; they ridicule him that is in affliction; they laugh at him that is in bonds.

Chapter VII.—Let us stand aloof from such heretics.

They abstain from the Eucharist and from prayer, because they confess not the Eucharist to be the flesh of our Savior Jesus Christ, which suffered for our sins, and which the Father, of His goodness, raised up again. Those, therefore, who speak against this gift of God, incur death in the midst of their disputes. But it were better for them to treat it with respect, that they also might rise again. It is fitting, therefore, that ye should keep aloof from such persons, and not to speak of them either in private or in public, but to give heed to the prophets, and above all, to the Gospel, in which the passion [of Christ] has been revealed to us, and the resurrection has been fully proved. But avoid all divisions, as the beginning of evils.

They are ashamed of the cross; they mock at the passion; they make a jest of the resurrection. They are the offspring of that spirit who is the author of all evil, who led Adam, by means of his wife, to transgress the commandment, who slew Abel by the hands of Cain, who fought against Job, who was the accuser of Joshua the son of Josedech, who sought to "sift the faith" of the apostles, who stirred up the multitude of the Jews against the Lord, who also now "worketh in the children of disobedience; from whom the Lord Jesus Christ will deliver us, who prayed that the faith of the apostles might not fail, not because He was not able of Himself to preserve it, but because He rejoiced in the pre-eminence of the Father. It is fitting, therefore, that ye should keep aloof from such persons, and neither in private nor in public to talk with them; but to give heed to the law, and the prophets, and to those who have preached to you the word of salvation. But flee from all abominable heresies, and those that cause schisms, as the beginning of evils.

Chapter VIII.—Let nothing be done without the bishop.

See that ye all follow the bishop, even as Jesus Christ does the Father, and the presbytery as ye would the apostles; and reverence the deacons, as being the institution of God. Let no man do anything connected with the Church without the bishop. Let that be deemed a proper Eucharist, which is [administered] either by the bishop, or by one to whom he has entrusted it. Wherever the bishop shall appear, there let the multitude [of the people] also be; even as, wherever Jesus Christ is, there is the Catholic Church. It is not lawful without the bishop either to baptize or to celebrate a love-feast; but whatsoever he shall approve of, that is also pleasing to God, so that everything that is done may be secure and valid.

See that ye all follow the bishop, even as Christ Jesus does the Father, and the presbytery as ye would the apostles. Do ye also reverence the deacons, as those that carry out [through their office] the appointment of God. Let no man do anything connected with the Church without the bishop. Let that be deemed a proper Eucharist, which is [administered] either by the bishop, or by one to whom he has entrusted it. Wherever the bishop shall appear, there let the multitude [of the people] also be; even as where Christ is, there does all the heavenly host stand by, waiting upon Him as the Chief Captain of the Lord's might, and the Governor of every intelligent nature. It is not lawful without the bishop either to baptize, or to offer, or to present sacrifice, or to celebrate a love-feast. But that which seems good to him, is also well-pleasing to God, that everything ye do may be secure and valid.

Chapter IX.—Honor the bishop.

Moreover, it is in accordance with reason that we should return to soberness [of conduct], and, while yet we have opportunity, exercise repentance towards God. It is well to reverence both God and the bishop. He who honors the bishop has been honored by God; he who does anything without the knowledge of the bishop, does [in reality] serve the devil. Let all things, then, abound to you through grace, for ye are worthy. Ye have refreshed me in all things, and Jesus Christ [shall refresh] you. Ye have loved me when absent as well as when present. May God recompense you, for whose sake, while ye endure all things, ye shall attain unto Him.

Moreover, it is in accordance with reason that we should return to soberness [of conduct], and, while yet we have opportunity, exercise repentance towards God. For "in Hades there is no one who can confess his sins." For "behold the man, and his work is before him." And [the Scripture saith], "My son, honor thou God and the king." And say I, Honor thou God indeed, as the Author and Lord of all things, but the bishop as the high-priest, who bears the image of God—of God, inasmuch as he is a ruler, and of Christ, in his capacity of a priest. After Him, we must also honor the king. For there is no one superior to God, or even like to Him, among all the beings that exist. Nor is there anyone in the Church greater than the bishop, who ministers as a priest to God for the salvation of the whole world. Nor, again, is there any one among rulers to be compared with the king, who secures peace and good order to those over whom he rules. He who honors the bishop shall be honored by God, even as he that dishonors him shall be punished by God. For if he that rises up against kings is justly held worthy of punishment, inasmuch as he dissolves public order, of how much sorer punishment, suppose ye, shall he be thought worthy, who presumes to do anything without the bishop, thus both destroying the [Church's] unity, and throwing its order into confusion? For the priesthood is the very highest point of all good things among men, against which whosoever is mad enough to strive, dishonors not man, but God, and Christ Jesus, the First-born, and the only High Priest, by nature, of the Father. Let all things therefore be done by you with good order in Christ. Let the laity be subject to the deacons; the deacons to the presbyters; the presbyters to the bishop; the bishop to Christ, even as He is to the Father. As ye, brethren, have refreshed me, so will Jesus Christ refresh you. Ye have loved me when absent, as well as when present. God will recompense you, for whose sake ye have shown such kindness towards His prisoner. For even if I am not worthy of it, yet your zeal [to help me] is an admirable thing. For "he who honors a prophet in the name of a prophet, shall receive a prophet's reward." It is manifest also, that he who honors a prisoner of Jesus Christ shall receive the reward of the martyrs.

Chapter X.—Acknowledgment of their kindness.

Ye have done well in receiving Philo and Rheus Agathopus as servants of Christ our God, who have followed me for the sake of God, and who give thanks to the Lord in your behalf, because ye have in every way refreshed them. None of these things shall be lost to you.

May my spirit be for you, and my bonds, which ye have not despised or been ashamed of; nor shall Jesus Christ, our perfect hope, be ashamed of you.

Ye have done well in receiving Philo, and Gaius, and Agathopus, who, being the servants of Christ, have followed me for the sake of God, and who greatly bless the Lord in your behalf, because ye have in every way refreshed them. None of those things which ye have done to them shall be passed by without being reckoned unto you. "The Lord grant" to you "that ye may find mercy of the Lord in that day!" May my spirit be for you, and my bonds, which ye have not despised or been ashamed of. Wherefore, neither shall Jesus Christ, our perfect hope, be ashamed of you.

Chapter XI.—Request to them to send a messenger to Antioch.

Your prayer has reached to the Church which is at Antioch in Syria. Coming from that place bound with chains, most acceptable to God, I salute all; I who am not worthy to be styled from thence, inasmuch as I am the least of them. Nevertheless, according to the will of God, I have been thought worthy [of this honor], not that I have any sense [of having deserved it], but by the grace of God, which I wish may be perfectly given to me, that through your prayers I may attain to God. In order, therefore, that your work may be complete both on earth and in heaven, it is fitting that, for the honor of God, your Church should elect some worthy delegate; so that he, journeying into Syria, may congratulate them that they are [now] at peace, and are restored to their proper greatness, and that their proper constitution has been re-established among them. It seems then to me a becoming thing, that you should send someone of your number with an epistle, so that, in company with them, he may rejoice569over the tranquility which, according to the will of God, they have obtained, and because that, through your prayers, they have now reached the harbor. As persons who are perfect, ye should also aim at those things which are perfect. For when ye are desirous to do well, God is also ready to assist you. Your prayers have reached to the Church of Antioch, and it is at peace. Coming from that place bound, I salute all; I who am not worthy to be styled from thence, inasmuch as I am the least of them. Nevertheless, according to the will of God, I have been thought worthy [of this honor], not that I have any sense [of having deserved it], but by the grace of God, which I wish may be perfectly given to me, that through your prayers I may attain to God. In order, therefore, that your work may be complete both on earth and in heaven, it is fitting that, for the honor of God, your Church should elect some worthy delegate; so that he, journeying into Syria, may congratulate them that they are [now] at peace, and are restored to their proper greatness, and that their proper constitution has been re-established among them. What appears to me proper to be done is this, that you should send someone of your number with an epistle, so that, in company with them, he may rejoice over the tranquility which, according to the will of God, they have obtained, and because that, through your prayers, I have secured Christ as a safe harbor. As persons who are perfect, ye should also aim at those things which are perfect. For when ye are desirous to do well, God is also ready to assist you.

Chapter XII.—Salutations.

The love of the brethren at Troas salutes you; whence also I write to you by Burrhus, whom ye sent with me, together with the Ephesians, your brethren, and who has in all things refreshed me. And I would that all may imitate him, as being a pattern of a minister of God. Grace will reward him in all things. I salute your most worthy bishop, and your very venerable presbytery, and your deacons, my fellow-servants, and all of you individually, as well as generally, in the name of Jesus Christ, and in His flesh and blood, in His passion and resurrection, both corporeal and spiritual, in union with God and you. Grace, mercy, peace, and patience, be with you for evermore!

The love of your brethren at Troas salutes you; whence also I write to you by Burgus, whom ye sent with me, together with the Ephesians, your brethren, and who has in all things refreshed me. And I would that all may imitate him, as being a pattern of a minister of God. The grace of the Lord will reward him in all things. I salute your most worthy bishop Polycarp, and your venerable presbytery, and your Christ-bearing deacons, my fellow-servants, and all of you individually, as well as generally, in the name of Christ Jesus, and in His flesh and blood, in His passion and resurrection, both corporeal and spiritual, in union with God and you. Grace, mercy, peace, and patience, be with you in Christ for evermore!

Chapter XIII.—Conclusion.

I salute the families of my brethren, with their wives and children, and the virgins who are called widows. Be ye strong, I pray, in the power of the Holy

Ghost. Philo, who is with me, greets you. I salute the house of Tavias, and pray that it may be confirmed in faith and love, both corporeal and spiritual. I salute Alce, my well-beloved, and the incomparable Daphnus, and Eutecnus, and all by name. Fare ye well in the grace of God.

I salute the families of my brethren, with their wives and children, and those that are ever virgins, and the widows. Be ye strong, I pray, in the power of the Holy Ghost. Philo, my fellow-servant, who is with me, greets you. I salute the house of Tavias, and pray that it may be confirmed in faith and love, both corporeal and spiritual. I salute Alce; my well-beloved, and the incomparable Daphnus, and Eutecnus, and all by name. Fare ye well in the grace of God, and of our Lord Jesus Christ, being filled with the Holy Spirit, and divine and sacred wisdom.

The Epistle of Ignatius to Polycarp Shorter and Longer Versions

Ignatius, who is also called Theophorus, to Polycarp, Bishop of the Church of the Smyrnæans, or rather, who has, as his own bishop, God the Father, and the Lord Jesus Christ: [wishes] abundance of happiness.

Ignatius, bishop of Antioch, and a witness for Jesus Christ, to Polycarp, Bishop of the Church of the Smyrnæans, or rather, who has, as his own bishop, God the Father, and Jesus Christ: [wishes] abundance of happiness.

Chapter I.—Commendation and exhortation.

Having obtained good proof that thy mind is fixed

in God as upon an immoveable rock, I loudly glorify [His name] that I have been thought worthy [to behold] thy blameless face, which may I ever enjoy in God! I entreat thee, by the grace with which thou art clothed, to press forward in thy course, and to exhort all that they may be saved. Maintain thy position with all care, both in the flesh and spirit. Have a regard to preserve unity, than which nothing is better. Bear with all, even as the Lord does with thee. Support all in love, as also thou does. Give thyself to prayer without ceasing. Implore additional understanding to what thou already hast. Be watchful, possessing a sleepless spirit. Speak to every man separately, as God enables thee. Bear the infirmities of all, as being a perfect athlete [in the Christian life]: where the labor is great, the gain is all the more.

Having obtained good proof that thy mind is fixed in God as upon an immoveable rock, I loudly glorify [His name] that I have been thought worthy to behold thy blameless face, which may I ever enjoy in God! I entreat thee, by the grace with which thou art clothed, to press forward in thy course, and to exhort all that they may be saved. Maintain thy position with all care, both in the flesh and spirit. Have a regard to preserve unity, than which nothing is better. Bear with all even as the Lord does with thee. Support all in love, as also thou does. Give thyself to prayer without ceasing. Implore additional understanding to what thou already hast. Be watchful, possessing a sleepless spirit. Speak to every man separately, as God enables thee. Bear the infirmities of all, as being a perfect athlete [in the Christian life], even as does the Lord of all. For says [the Scripture], "He Himself took our infirmities, and bare our sicknesses." Where the labor is great, the gain is all the more.

St. Ignatius

Chapter II.—Exhortations.

If thou loves the good disciples, no thanks are due to thee on that account; but rather seek by meekness to subdue the more troublesome. Every kind of wound is not healed with the same plaster. Mitigate violent attacks [of disease] by gentle applications. Be in all things "wise as a serpent, and harmless as a dove." For this purpose thou art composed of both flesh and spirit, that thou mayest deal tenderly with those [evils] that present themselves visibly before thee. And as respects those that are not seen, pray that [God] would reveal them unto thee, in order that thou mayest be wanting in nothing, but mayest abound in every gift. The times call for thee, as pilots do for the winds, and as one tossed with tempest seeks for the haven, so that both thou [and those under thy care] may attain to God. Be sober as an athlete of God: the prize set before thee is immortality and eternal life, of which thou art also persuaded. In all things may my soul be for thine, and my bonds also, which thou hast loved.

If thou loves the good disciples, no thanks are due to thee on that account; but rather seek by meekness to subdue the more troublesome. Every kind of wound is not healed with the same plaster. Mitigate violent attacks [of disease] by gentle applications. Be in all things "wise as a serpent, and harmless always as a dove." For this purpose thou art composed of both soul and body, art both fleshly and spiritual, that thou mayest correct those [evils] that present themselves visibly before thee; and as respects those that are not seen, mayest pray that these should be revealed to thee, so that thou mayest be wanting in nothing, but mayest abound in every gift. The times call upon thee to pray. For as the wind aids the pilot of a ship, and as havens are advantageous for safety to a tempest-tossed vessel, so is also prayer to thee, in order that thou mayest attain to God. Be sober as an athlete of God, whose will is immortality and eternal life; of which thou art also persuaded. In all things may my soul be for thine, and my bonds also, which thou hast loved.

Chapter III.—Exhortations.

Let not those who seem worthy of credit, but teach strange doctrines, fill thee with apprehension. Stand firm, as does an anvil which is beaten. It is the part of a noble athlete to be wounded, and yet to conquer. And especially, we ought to bear all things for the sake of God, that He also may bear with us. Be ever becoming more zealous than what thou art. Weigh carefully the times. Look for Him who is above all time, eternal and invisible, yet who became visible for our sakes; impalpable and impassible, yet who became passible on our account; and who in every kind of way suffered for our sakes.

Let not those who seem worthy of credit, but teach strange doctrines, fill thee with apprehension. Stand firm, as does an anvil which is beaten. It is the part of a noble athlete to be wounded, and yet to conquer. And especially we ought to bear all things for the sake of God, that He also may bear with us, and bring us into His kingdom. Add more and more to thy diligence; run thy race with increasing energy; weigh carefully the times. Whilst thou art here, be a conqueror; for here is the course, and there are the crowns. Look for Christ, the Son of God; who was before time, yet appeared in time; who was invisible by nature, yet visible in the flesh; who was impalpable, and could not be touched, as being without a body, but for our sakes became such, might be touched and handled in the body; who was impassible as God, but became passible for our sakes as man; and who in every kind of way suffered for our sakes.

Chapter IV.—Exhortations.

Let not widows be neglected. Be thou, after the Lord, their protector and friend. Let nothing be done without thy consent; neither do thou anything without the approval of God, which indeed thou dost not, inasmuch as thou art steadfast. Let your assembling together be of frequent occurrence: seek after all by name. Do not despise either male or female slaves, yet neither let them be puffed up with conceit, but rather let them submit themselves the more, for the glory of God, that they may obtain from God a better liberty. Let them not long to be set free [from slavery] at the public expense, that they be not found slaves to their own desires.

Let not the widows be neglected. Be thou, after the Lord, their protector and friend. Let nothing be done without thy consent; neither do thou anything without the approval of God, which indeed thou does not. Be thou steadfast. Let your assembling together be of frequent occurrence: seek after all by name. Do not despise either male or female slaves, yet neither let them be puffed up with conceit, but rather let them submit themselves the more, for the glory of God, that they may obtain from God a better liberty. Let them not wish to be set free [from slavery] at the public expense, that they be not found slaves to their own desires.

Chapter V.—The duties of husbands and wives.

Flee evil arts; but all the more discourse in public regarding them. Speak to my sisters, that they love the Lord, and be satisfied with their husbands both in the flesh and spirit. In like manner also, exhort my brethren, in the name of Jesus Christ, that they love their wives, even as the Lord the Church. If anyone can continue in a state of purity, to the honor of Him who is Lord of the flesh, let him so remain without boasting. If he begins to boast, he is undone; and if he reckon himself greater than the bishop, he is ruined. But it becomes both men and women who marry, to form their union with the approval of the bishop, that their marriage may be according to God, and not after their own lust. Let all things be done to the honor of God. Flee evil arts; but all the more discourse in public regarding them. Speak to my sisters, that they love the Lord, and be satisfied with their husbands both in the flesh and spirit. In like manner also, exhort my brethren, in the name of Jesus Christ, that they love their wives, even as the Lord the Church. If anyone can continue in a state of purity, to the honor of the flesh of the Lord, let him so remain without boasting. If he shall boast, he is undone; and if he seeks to be more prominent than the bishop, he is ruined. But it becomes both men and women who marry, to form their union with the approval of the bishop, that their marriage may be according to the Lord, and not after their own lust. Let all things be done to the honor of God.

Chapter VI.—The duties of the Christian flock.

Give ye heed to the bishop, that God also may

give heed to you. My soul be for theirs that are submissive to the bishop, to the presbyters, and to the deacons, and may my portion be along with them in God! Labor together with one another; strive in company together; run together; suffer together; sleep together; and awake together, as the stewards, and associates, and servants of God. Please ye Him under whom ye fight, and from whom ye receive your wages. Let none of you be found a deserter. Let your baptism endure as your arms; your faith as your helmet; your love as your spear; your patience as a complete panoply. Let your works be the charge assigned to you, that ye may receive a worthy recompense. Be long-suffering, therefore, with one another, in meekness, as God is towards you. May I have joy of you forever! Give ye heed to the bishop, that God also may give heed to you. My soul be for theirs that are submissive to the bishop, to the presbytery, and to the deacons: may I have my portion with them from God! Labor together with one another; strive in company together; run together; suffer together; sleep together; and awake together, as the stewards, and associates, and servants of God. Please ye Him under whom ye fight, and from whom ye shall receive your wages. Let none of you be found a deserter. Let your baptism endure as your arms; your faith as your helmet; your love as your spear; your patience as a complete panoply. Let your works be the charge assigned to you, that you may obtain for them a most worthy recompense. Be long-suffering, therefore, with one another, in meekness, and God shall be so with you. May I have joy of you forever!

Chapter VII.—Request that Polycarp would send a messenger to Antioch.

Seeing that the Church which is at Antioch in Syria is, as report has informed me, at peace, through your prayers, I also am the more encouraged, resting without anxiety in God, if indeed by means of suffering I may attain to God, so that, through your prayers, I may be found a disciple [of Christ]. It is fitting, O Polycarp, most blessed in God, to assemble a very solemn council, and to elect one whom you greatly love, and know to be a man of activity, who may be designated the messenger of God; and to bestow on him this honor that he may go into Syria, and glorify your ever active love to the praise of Christ. A Christian has not power over himself, but must always be ready for the service of God. Now, this work is both God's and yours, when ye shall have completed it to His glory. For I trust that, through grace, ye are prepared for every good work pertaining to God. Knowing, therefore, your energetic love of the truth, I have exhorted you by this brief Epistle.

Seeing that the Church which is at Antioch in Syria is, as report has informed me, at peace, through your prayers, I also am the more encouraged, resting without anxiety in God, if indeed by means of suffering I may attain to God, so that, through your prayers, I may be found a disciple [of Christ]. It is fitting, O Polycarp, most blessed in God, to assemble a very solemn council, and to elect one whom you greatly love, and know to be a man of activity, who may be designated the messenger of God; and to bestow on him the honor of going into Syria, so that, going into Syria, he may glorify your ever active love to the praise of God. A Christian has not power over himself, but must always be ready for the service of God. Now, this work is both God's and yours, when ye shall have completed it. For I trust that, through grace, ye are prepared for every good work pertaining to God. Knowing your energetic love of the truth, I have exhorted you by this brief Epistle.

Chapter VIII.—Let other churches also send to Antioch.

Inasmuch as I have not been able to write to all the Churches, because I must suddenly sail from Troas to Neapolis, as the will [of the emperor] enjoins, [I beg that] thou, as being acquainted with the purpose of God, wilt write to the adjacent Churches, that they also may act in like manner, such as are able to do so sending messengers, and the others transmitting letters through those persons who are sent by thee, that thou mayest be glorified by a work which shall be remembered for ever, as indeed thou art worthy to be. I salute all by name, and in particular the wife of Epitropus, with all her house and children. I salute Attalus, my beloved. I salute him who shall be deemed worthy to go [from you] into Syria. Grace shall be with him forever, and with Polycarp that sends him. I pray for your happiness forever in our God, Jesus Christ, by whom continue ye in the unity and under the protection of God, I salute Alce, my dearly beloved. Fare ye well in the Lord.

Inasmuch, therefore, as I have not been able to write to all Churches, because I must suddenly sail from Troas to Neapolis, as the will [of the emperor] enjoins, [I beg that] thou, as being acquainted with the purpose of God, wilt write to the adjacent Churches, that they also

The Epistles of St. Ignatius

may act in like manner, such as are able to do so sending messenger, and the others transmitting letters through those persons who are sent by thee, that thou mayest be glorified by a work which shall be remembered for ever, as indeed thou art worthy to be. I salute all by name, and in particular the wife of Epitropus, with all her house and children. I salute Attalus, my beloved. I salute him who shall be deemed worthy to go [from you] into Syria. Grace shall be with him forever, and with Polycarp that sends him. I pray for your happiness forever in our God, Jesus Christ, by whom continue you in the unity and under the protection of God. I salute Alce, my dearly beloved. Amen. Grace [be with you]. Fare ye well in the Lord.

Introductory Note to the Syriac Version of the Ignatian Epistles

When the Syriac version of the Ignatian Epistles was introduced to the English world in 1845, by Mr. Cureton, the greatest satisfaction was expressed by many, who thought the inveterate controversy about to be settled. Lord Russell made the learned divine a canon of Westminster Abbey, and the critical Chevalier Bunsen committed himself as its patron. To the credit of the learned, in general, the work was gratefully received, and studied with scientific conscientiousness by Lightfoot and others. The literature of this period is valuable; and the result is decisive as to the Curetonian versions at least, which are fragmentary and abridged, and yet they are a valuable contribution to the study of the whole case. The following is the original Introductory Notice:— Some account of the discovery of the Syriac version of the

Ignatian Epistles has been already given. We have simply to add here a brief description of the mss. from which the Syriac text has been printed. That which is named α by Cureton, contains only the Epistle to Polycarp, and exhibits the text of that Epistle which, after him, we have followed. He fixes its age somewhere in the first half of the sixth century, or before the year 550. The second ms., which Cureton refers to as β, is assigned by him to the seventh or eighth century. It contains the three Epistles of Ignatius, and furnishes the text here followed in the Epistles to the Ephesians and Romans. The third ms., which Cureton quotes as γ, has no date, but, as he tells us, "belonged to the collection acquired by Moses of Nisibis in a.d.931, and was written apparently about three or four centuries earlier." It contains the three Epistles to Polycarp, the Ephesians, and the Romans. The text of all these mss. is in several passages manifestly corrupt, and the translators appear at times to have mistaken the meaning of the Greek original. [N.B.—Bunsen is forced to allow the fact that the discovery of the lost work of Hippolytus "throws new light on an obscure point of the Ignatian controversy," i.e., the Sige in the Epistle to the Magnesians (cap. viii.); but his treatment of the matter is unworthy of a candid scholar.]

The Epistle of Ignatius to Polycarp

Ignatius, who is [also called] Theophorus, to Polycarp, bishop of Smyrna, or rather, who has as his own bishop God the Father, and our Lord Jesus Christ: [wishes] abundance of happiness.

Chapter I.

Because thy mind is acceptable to me, inasmuch as it is established in God, as on a rock which is immoveable, I glorify God the more exceedingly that I have been counted worthy of [seeing] thy face, which I longed after in God. Now I beseech thee, by the grace with which thou art clothed, to add [speed] to thy course, and that thou ever pray for all men that they may be saved, and that thou demand things which are befitting, with all assiduity both of the flesh and spirit. Be studious of unity, than which nothing is more precious. Bear with all men, even as our Lord beareth with thee. Show patience with all men in love, as [indeed] thou does. Be steadfast in prayer. Ask for more understanding than that which thou [already] hast. Be watchful, as possessing a spirit which sleepeth not. Speak with every man according to the will of God. Bear the infirmities of all men as a perfect athlete; for where the labor is great, the gain is also great.

Chapter II.

If thou loves the good disciples only, thou hast no grace; [but] rather subdue those that are evil by gentleness. All [sorts of] wounds are not healed by the same medicine. Mitigate [the pain of] cutting by tenderness. Be wise as the serpent in everything, and innocent, with respect to those things which are requisite, even as the dove. For this reason thou art [composed] of both flesh and spirit, that thou mayest entice those things which are visible before thy face, and mayest ask, as to those which are concealed from thee, that they [too] may be revealed to thee, in order that thou be deficient in nothing, and mayest abound in all gifts. The time demands, even as a pilot does a ship, and as one who stands exposed to the tempest does a haven, that thou should be worthy of God. Be thou watchful as an athlete of God. That which is promised to us is life eternal, which cannot be corrupted, of which things thou art also persuaded. In everything I will be instead of thy soul, and my bonds which thou hast loved.

Chapter III.

Let not those who seem to be somewhat, and teach strange doctrines, strike thee with apprehension; but stand thou in the truth, as an athlete who is smitten, for it is [the part] of a great athlete to be smitten, and [yet] conquer. More especially is it fitting that we should bear everything for the sake of God, that He also may bear us. Be [still] more diligent than thou yet art. Be discerning of the times. Look for Him that is above the times, Him who has no times, Him who is invisible, Him who for our sakes became visible, Him who is impalpable, Him who is impassible, Him who for our sakes suffered, Him who endured everything in every form for our sakes.

Chapter IV.

Let not the widows be overlooked; on account of our Lord be thou their guardian, and let nothing be done without thy will; also do thou nothing without the will of God, as indeed thou does not. Stand rightly. Let there be frequent assemblies: ask every man [to them] by his name. Despise not slaves, either male or female; but neither let them be contemptuous, but let them labor the more as for the glory of God, that they may be counted worthy of a more precious freedom, which is of God. Let them not desire to be set free out of the common [fund], lest they be found the slaves of lust.

Chapter V.

Flee wicked arts; but all the more discourse regarding them. Speak to my sisters, that they love in our Lord, and that their husbands be sufficient for them in the flesh and spirit. Then, again, charge my brethren in the name of our Lord Jesus Christ, that they love their wives, as our Lord His Church. If any man is able in power to continue in purity, to the honor of the flesh of our Lord, let him continue so without boasting; if he boasts, he is undone; if he become known apart from the bishop, he has destroyed himself. It is becoming, therefore, to men and women who marry, that they marry with the counsel of the bishop, that the marriage may be in our Lord, and not in lust. Let everything, therefore, be [done] for the honor of God.

Chapter VI.

Look you to the bishop, that God also may look upon you. I will be instead of the souls of those who are subject to the bishop, and the presbyters, and the deacons; with them may I have a portion in the presence of God! Labor together with one another, act as athletes together, run together, suffer together, sleep together, rise together. As stewards of God, and of His household, and His servants, please Him and serve Him, that ye may receive from Him the wages [promised]. Let none of you be rebellious. Let your baptism be to you as armor, and faith as a spear, and love as a helmet, and patience as a panoply. Let your treasures be your good works, that ye may receive the gift of God, as is just. Let your spirit be long-suffering towards each other with meekness, even as God [is] toward you. As for me, I rejoice in you at all times.

Chapter VII.

The Christian has not power over himself, but is [ever] ready to be subject to God.

Chapter VIII.

I salute him who is reckoned worthy to go to Antioch in my stead, as I commanded thee.

The Second Epistle of Ignatius to the Ephesians

Ignatius, who is [also called] Theophorus, to the Church which is blessed in the greatness of God the Father, and perfected; to her who was selected from eternity, that she might be at all times for glory, which abided, and is unchangeable, and is perfected and chosen in the purpose of truth by the will of the Father of Jesus Christ our God; to her who is worthy of happiness; to her who is at Ephesus, in Jesus Christ, in joy which is unblameable: [wishes] abundance of happiness.

Chapter I.

Inasmuch as your name, which is greatly beloved, is acceptable to me in God, [your name] which ye have acquired by nature, through a right and just will, and also by the faith and love of Jesus Christ our Savior, and ye are imitators of God, and are fervent in the blood of God, and have speedily completed a work congenial to you; [for] when ye heard that I was bound, so as to be able to do nothing for the sake of the common name and hope (and I hope, through your prayers, that I may be devoured by beasts at Rome, so that by means of this of which I have been accounted worthy, I may be endowed with strength to be a disciple of God), ye were diligent to come and see me. Seeing, then, that we have become acquainted with your multitude in the name of God, by Onesimus, who is your bishop, in love which is unutterable, whom I pray that ye love in Jesus Christ our Lord, and that all of you imitate his example, for blessed is He who has given you such a bishop, even as ye deserve [to have].

Chapter III.

But inasmuch as love does not permit me to be silent in regard to you, on this account I have been forward to entreat of you that ye would be diligent in the will of God.

Chapter VIII.

For, so long as there is not implanted in you any one lust which is able to torment you, behold, ye live in

God. I rejoice in you, and offer supplication on account of you, Ephesians, a Church which is renowned in all ages. For those who are carnal are not able to do spiritual things, nor those that are spiritual carnal things; in like manner as neither can faith [do] those things which are foreign to faith, nor want of faith [do] what belongs to faith. For those things which ye have done in the flesh, even these are spiritual, because ye have done everything in Jesus Christ.

Chapter IX.

And ye are prepared for the building of God the Father, and ye are raised up on high by the instrument of Jesus Christ, which is the cross; and ye are drawn by the rope, which is the Holy Spirit; and your pulley is your faith, and your love is the way which leaded up on high to God.

Chapter X.

Pray for all men; for there is hope of repentance for them, that they may be counted worthy of God. By your works especially let them be instructed. Against their harsh words be ye conciliatory, by meekness of mind and gentleness. Against their blasphemies do ye give yourselves to prayer; and against their error be ye armed with faith. Against their fierceness be ye peaceful and quiet, and be ye not astounded by them. Let us, then, be imitators of our Lord in meekness, and strive who shall more especially be injured, and oppressed, and defrauded.

Chapter XIV.

The work is not of promise, unless a man be found in the power of faith, even to the end.

Chapter XV.

It is better that a man should be silent while he is something, than that he should be talking when he is not; that by those things which he speaks he should act, and by those things of which he is silent he should be known.

Chapter XVIII.

My spirit bows in adoration to the cross, which is a stumbling-block to those who do not believe, but is to you for salvation and eternal life.

Chapter XIX.

There was concealed from the ruler of this world the virginity of Mary and the birth of our Lord, and the three renowned mysteries which were done in the tranquility of God from the star. And here, at the manifestation of the Son, magic began to be destroyed, and all bonds were loosed; and the ancient kingdom and the error of evil was destroyed. Henceforward all things were moved together, and the destruction of death was devised, and there was the commencement of that which was perfected in God.

The Third Epistle of the Same St. Ignatius

Ignatius, who is [also called] Theophorus, to the Church which has received grace through the greatness of the Father Most High; to her who presides in the place of the region of the Romans, who is worthy of God, and worthy of life, and happiness, and praise, and remembrance, and is worthy of prosperity, and presides in love, and is perfected in the law of Christ unblameable: [wishes] abundance of peace.

Chapter I.

From of old have I prayed to God, that I might be counted worthy to behold your faces which are worthy of God: now, therefore, being bound in Jesus Christ, I hope to meet you and salute you, if it be the will [of God] that I should be accounted worthy to the end. For the beginning is well arranged, if I be counted worthy to attain to the end, that I may receive my portion, without hindrance, through suffering. For I am in fear of your love, lest it should injure me. As to you, indeed, it is easy for you to do whatsoever ye wish; but as to me, it is difficult for me to be accounted worthy of God, if indeed ye spare me not.

Chapter II.

For there is no other time such as this, that I should be accounted worthy of God; neither will ye, if ye be silent, [ever] be found in a better work than this. If ye let me alone, I shall be the word of God; but if ye love my flesh, again am I [only] to myself a voice. Ye cannot give me anything more precious than this, that I should be sacrificed to God, while the altar is ready; that ye may be in one concord in love, and may praise God the Father through Jesus Christ our Lord, because He has deemed a bishop worthy to be God's, having called him from the east to the west. It is good that I should set from the world in God, that I may rise in Him to life.

Chapter III.

Ye have never envied any man. Ye have taught others. Only pray ye for strength to be given to me from within and from without, that I may not only speak, but also may be willing, and that I may not merely be called a Christian, but also may be found to be [one]; for if I am found to be [so], I may then also be called [so]. Then [indeed] shall I be faithful, when I am no longer seen in the world. For there is nothing visible that is good. The work is not [a matter] of persuasion; but Christianity is great when the world hateth it.

Chapter IV.

I write to all the Churches, and declare to all men, that I willingly die for the sake of God, if so be that ye hinder me not. I entreat of you not to be [affected] towards me with a love which is unseasonable. Leave me to become [the prey of] the beasts, that by their means I may be accounted worthy of God. I am the wheat of God, and by the teeth of the beasts I shall be ground, that I may be found the pure bread of God. Provoke you greatly the wild beasts, that they may be for me a grave, and may leave nothing of my body, in order that, when I have fallen asleep, I may not be a burden upon any one. Then shall I be in truth a disciple of Jesus Christ, when the world seeth not even my body. Entreat of our Lord in my behalf, that through these instruments I may be found a sacrifice to God. I do not, like Peter and Paul, issue orders unto you. They are apostles, but I am one condemned; they indeed are free, but I am a slave, even until now. But if I suffer, I shall be the freed-man of Jesus Christ, and I shall rise in Him from the dead, free. And now being in bonds, I learn to desire nothing.

Chapter V.

From Syria, and even unto Rome, I am cast among wild beasts, by sea and by land, by night and by day, being bound between ten leopards, which are the band of soldiers, who, even when I do good to them, all the more do evil unto me. I, however, am the rather instructed by their injurious treatment; but not on this account am I justified to myself. I rejoice in the beasts which are prepared for me, and I pray that they may in haste be found for me; and I will provoke them speedily to devour me, and not be as those which are afraid of some other men, and will not approach them: even should they not be willing to approach me, I will go with violence against them. Know me from myself what is expedient for me. Let no one envy me of those things which are seen and which are not seen, that I should be accounted worthy of Jesus Christ. Fire, and the cross, and the beasts that are prepared, cutting off of the limbs, and scattering of the bones, and crushing of the whole body, harsh torments of the devil—let these come upon me, but only let me be accounted worthy of Jesus Christ.

Chapter VI.

The pains of the birth stand over against me.

Chapter VII.

And my love is crucified, and there is no fire in me for another love. I do not desire the food of corruption, neither the lusts of this world. I seek the bread of God, which is the flesh of Jesus Christ; and I seek His blood, a drink which is love incorruptible.

Chapter IX.

My spirit salutes you, and the love of the Churches which received me as the name of Jesus Christ; for those also who were near to [my] way in the flesh, preceded me in every city.

[Now therefore, being about to arrive shortly in Rome, I know many things in God; but I keep myself within measure, that I may not perish through boasting: for now it is needful for me to fear the more, and not pay regard to those who puff me up. For they who say such things to me scourge me; for I desire to suffer, but I do not know if I am worthy. For zeal is not visible to many, but with me it has war. I have need, therefore, of meekness, by which the prince of this world is destroyed. I am able to write to you of heavenly things, but I fear lest I should do you an injury. Know me from myself. For I am cautious lest ye should not be able to receive [such knowledge], and should be perplexed. For even I, not because I am in bonds, and am able to know heavenly things, and the places of angels, and the stations of the powers that are seen and that are not seen, am on this account a disciple; for I am far short of the perfection which is worthy of God.] Be ye perfectly strong in the patience of Jesus Christ our God.

Here end the three Epistles of Ignatius, bishop and martyr.

Introductory Note to the Spurious Epistles of Ignatius

To the following introductory note of the translators nothing need be prefixed, except a grateful acknowledgment of the value of their labors and of their good judgment in giving us even these spurious writings for purposes of comparison. They have thus placed the materials for a complete understanding of the whole subject, before students who have a mind to subject it to a thorough and candid examination.

The following is the original Introductory Notice:—

We formerly stated that eight out of the fifteen Epistles bearing the name of Ignatius are now universally admitted to be spurious. None of them are quoted or referred to by any ancient writer previous to the sixth century. The style, moreover, in which they are written, so different from that of the other Ignatian letters, and allusions which they contain to heresies and ecclesiastical arrangements of a much later date than that of their professed author, render it perfectly certain that they are not the authentic production of the illustrious bishop of Antioch.

We cannot tell when or by whom these Epistles

were fabricated. They have been thought to betray the same hand as the longer and interpolated form of the seven Epistles which are generally regarded as genuine. And some have conceived that the writer who gave forth to the world the Apostolic Constitutions under the name of Clement, was probably the author of these letters falsely ascribed to Ignatius, as well as of the longer recension of the seven Epistles which are mentioned by Eusebius.

It was a considerable time before editors in modern times began to discriminate between the true and the false in the writings attributed to Ignatius. The letters first published under his name were those three which exist only in Latin. These came forth in 1495 at Paris, being appended to a life of Becket, Archbishop of Canterbury. Some three years later, eleven Epistles, comprising those mentioned by Eusebius, and four others, were published in Latin, and passed through four or five editions. In 1536, the whole of the professedly Ignatian letters were published at Cologne in a Latin version; and this collection also passed through several editions. It was not till 1557 that the Ignatian Epistles appeared for the first time in Greek at Dillingen. After this date many editions came forth, in which the probably genuine were still mixed up with the certainly spurious, the three Latin letters, only being rejected as destitute of authority. Vedelius of Geneva first made the distinction which is now universally accepted, in an edition of these Epistles which he published in 1623; and he was followed by Archbishop Usher and others, who entered more fully into that critical examination of these writings which has been continued down even to our own day.

The reader will have no difficulty in detecting the

internal grounds on which these eight letters are set aside as spurious. The difference of style from the other Ignatian writings will strike him even in perusing the English version which we have given, while it is of course much more marked in the original. And other decisive proofs present themselves in every one of the Epistles. In that to the Tarsians there is found a plain allusion to the Sabellian heresy, which did not arise till after the middle of the third century. In the Epistle to the Antiochians there is an enumeration of various Church officers, who were certainly unknown at the period when Ignatius lived. The Epistle to Hero plainly alludes to Manichæan errors, and could not therefore have been written before the third century. There are equally decisive proofs of spuriousness to be found in the Epistle to the Philippians, such as the references it contains to the Patripassian heresy originated by Praxeas in the latter part of the second century, and the ecclesiastical feasts, etc., of which it makes mention. The letter to Maria Cassobolita is of a very peculiar style, utterly alien from that of the other Epistles ascribed to Ignatius. And it is sufficient simply to glance at the short Epistles to St. John and the Virgin Mary, in order to see that they carry the stamp of imposture on their front; and, indeed, no sooner were they published than by almost universal consent they were rejected.

But though the additional Ignatian letters here given are confessedly spurious, we have thought it not improper to present them to the English reader in an appendix to our first volume. We have done so, because they have been so closely connected with the name of the bishop of Antioch, and also because they are in themselves not destitute of interest. We have, moreover, the satisfaction of thus placing for the first time within the reach of one acquainted only with our language, all the materials that have entered into the protracted agitation of the famous Ignatian controversy.

The Epistle of Ignatius to the Tarsians

Ignatius, who is also called Theophorus, to the Church which is at Tarsus, saved in Christ, worthy of praise, worthy of remembrance, and worthy of love: Mercy and peace from God the Father, and the Lord Jesus Christ, be ever multiplied.

Chapter I.—His own sufferings: exhortation to steadfastness.

From Syria even unto Rome I fight with beasts: not that I am devoured by brute beasts, for these, as ye know, by the will of God, spared Daniel, but by beasts in the shape of men, in whom the merciless wild beast himself lies hid, and pricks and wounds me day by day. But none of these hardships "move me, neither count I my life dear unto myself," in such a way as to love it better than the Lord. Wherefore I am prepared for [encountering] fire, wild beasts, the sword or the cross, so that only I may see Christ my Savior and God, who died for me. I therefore, the prisoner of Christ, who am driven along by land and sea, exhort you: "stand fast in the faith," and be ye steadfast, "for the just shall live by faith;" be ye unwavering, for "the Lord causes those to dwell in a house who are of one and the same character."

Chapter II.—Cautions against false doctrine.

I have learned that certain of the ministers of Satan have wished to disturb you, some of them asserting that Jesus was born [only] in appearance, was crucified in appearance, and died in appearance; others that He is not the Son the Creator, and others that He is Himself God over all. Others, again, hold that He is a mere man, and others that this flesh is not to rise again, so that our proper course is to live and partake of a life of pleasure, for that this is the chief good to beings who are in a little while to perish. A swarm of such evils has burst in upon us. But ye have not "given place by subjection to them, no, not for one hour." For ye are the fellow-citizens as well as the disciples of Paul, who "fully preached the Gospel from Jerusalem, and round about unto Illyricum," and bare about "the marks of Christ" in his flesh.

Chapter III.—The true doctrine respecting Christ.

Mindful of him, do ye by all means know that Jesus the Lord was truly born of Mary, being made of a woman; and was as truly crucified. For, says he, "God forbid that I should glory, save in the cross of the Lord Jesus." And He really suffered, and died, and rose again. For says [Paul], "If Christ should become passible, and should be the first to rise again from the dead." And again, "In that He died, He died unto sin once: but in that He lives, He lives unto God." Otherwise, what advantage would there be in [becoming subject to] bonds, if Christ has not died? What advantage in patience? What advantage in [enduring] stripes? And why such facts as the following: Peter was crucified; Paul and James were slain with the sword; John was banished to Patmos; Stephen was stoned to death by the Jews who killed the

Lord? But, [in truth,] none of these sufferings were in vain; for the Lord was really crucified by the ungodly.

Chapter IV.—Continuation.

And [know ye, moreover], that He who was born of a woman was the Son of God, and He that was crucified was "the first-born of every creature," and God the Word, who also created all things. For says the apostle, "There is one God, the Father, of whom are all things; and one Lord Jesus Christ, by whom are all things." And again, "For there is one God, and one Mediator between God and man, the man Christ Jesus;" and, "By Him were all things created that are in heaven, and on earth, visible and invisible; and He is before all things, and by Him all things consist."

Chapter V.—Refutation of the previously mentioned errors.

And that He Himself is not God over all, and the Father, but His Son, He [shows when He] says, "I ascend unto my Father and your Father, and to my God and your God." And again, "When all things shall be subdued unto Him, then shall He also Himself be subject unto Him that put all things under Him, that God may be all in all." Wherefore it is one [Person] who put all things under, and who is all in all, and another [Person] to whom they were subdued, who also Himself, along with all other things, becomes subject [to the former].

Chapter VI.—Continuation.

Nor is He a mere man, by whom and in whom all things were made; for "all things were made by Him." "When He made the heaven, I was present with Him; and I was there with Him, forming [the world along with Him], and He rejoiced in me daily." And how could a mere man be addressed in such words as these: "Sit Thou at My right hand?" And how, again, could such a one declare: "Before Abraham was, I am?" And, "Glorify Me with Thy glory which I had before the world was?" What man could ever say, "I came down from heaven, not to do Mine own will, but the will of Him that sent Me?" And of what man could it be said, "He was the true Light, which lighted every man that cometh into the world: He was in the world, and the world was made by Him, and the world knew Him not. He came unto His own, and His own received Him not?" How could such a one be a mere man, receiving the beginning of His existence from Mary, and not rather God the Word, and the only-begotten Son? For "in the beginning was the Word, and the Word was with God, and the Word was God." And in another place, "The Lord created Me, the beginning of His ways, for His ways, for His works. Before the world did He found Me, and before all the hills did He beget Me."

Chapter VII.—Continuation.

And that our bodies are to rise again, He shows when He says, "Verily I say unto you, that the hour cometh, in the which all that are in the graves shall hear the voice of the Son of God; and they that hear shall live." And [says] the apostle, "For this corruptible must put on incorruption, and this mortal must put on immortality." And that we must live soberly and righteously, he [shows when he] says again, "Be not deceived: neither adulterers, nor effeminate persons, nor abusers of themselves with mankind, nor fornicators, nor revilers, nor drunkards, nor thieves, can inherit the kingdom of God." And again, "If the dead rise not, then is not Christ raised; our preaching therefore is vain, and your faith is also vain: ye are yet in your sins. Then they also that are fallen asleep in Christ have perished. If in this life only we have hope in Christ, we are of all men most miserable. If the dead rise not, let us eat and drink, for to-morrow we die." But if such be our condition and feelings, wherein shall we differ from asses and dogs, who have no care about the future, but think only of eating, and of indulging such appetites as follow after eating? For they are unacquainted with any intelligence moving within them.

Chapter VIII.—Exhortations to holiness and good order.

May I have joy of you in the Lord! Be ye sober. Lay aside, every one of you, all malice and beast-like fury, evil-speaking, calumny, filthy speaking, ribaldry, whispering, arrogance, drunkenness, lust, avarice, vainglory, envy, and everything akin to these. "But put you on the Lord Jesus Christ, and make no provision for the flesh, to fulfil the lusts thereof." Ye presbyters, be subject to the bishop; you deacons, to the presbyters; and you, the people, to the presbyters and the deacons. Let my soul be for theirs who preserve this good order; and may the Lord be with them continually!

Chapter IX.—Exhortations to the discharge of relative duties.

Ye husbands, love your wives; and ye wives, your husbands. Ye children, reverence your parents. Ye parents, "bring up your children in the nurture and admonition of the Lord." Honor those [who continue] in virginity, as the priestesses of Christ; and the widows [that persevere] in gravity of behavior, as the altar of God. Ye servants, wait upon your masters with [respectful] fear. Ye masters, issue orders to your servants with tenderness. Let no one among you be idle; for idleness is the mother of want. I do not enjoin these things as being a person of any consequence, although I am in bonds [for Christ]; but as a brother, I put you in mind of them. The Lord be with you!

Chapter X.—Salutations.

May I enjoy your prayers! Pray ye that may attain to Jesus. I commend unto you the Church which is at Antioch. The Churches of Philippi, whence also I write to you, salute you. Philo, your deacon, to whom also I give thanks as one who has zealously ministered to me in all things, salutes you. Agathopus, the deacon from Syria, who follows me in Christ, salutes you. "Salute ye one another with a holy kiss." I salute you all, both male and female, who are in Christ. Fare ye well in body, and soul, and in one Spirit; and do not ye forget me. The Lord be with you!

The Epistle of Ignatius to the Antiochians

Ignatius, who is also called Theophorus, to the Church sojourning in Syria, which has obtained mercy from God, and been elected by Christ, and which first received the name Christ, [wishes] happiness in God the Father, and the Lord Jesus Christ.

Chapter I.—Cautions against error.

The Lord has rendered my bonds light and easy since I learnt that you are in peace, that you live in all harmony both of the flesh and spirit. "I therefore, the prisoner of the Lord, beseech you, that ye walk worthy of the vocation wherewith ye are called," guarding against those heresies of the wicked one which have broken in upon us, to the deceiving and destruction of those that accept of them; but that ye give heed to the doctrine of the apostles, and believe both the law and the prophets: that ye reject every Jewish and Gentile error, and neither introduce a multiplicity of gods, nor yet deny Christ under the presence of [maintaining] the unity of God.

Chapter II.—The true doctrine respecting God and Christ.

For Moses, the faithful servant of God, when he said, "The Lord thy God is one Lord," and thus proclaimed that there was only one God, did yet forthwith confess also our Lord when he said, "The Lord rained upon Sodom and Gomorrah fire and brimstone from the Lord." And again, "And God said, Let Us make man after our image: and so God made man, after the image of God made He him." And further "In the image of God made He man." And that [the Son of God] was to be made man [Moses shows when] he says, "A prophet shall the Lord raise up unto you of your brethren, like unto me."

Chapter III.—The same continued.

The prophets also, when they speak as in the person of God, [saying,] "I am God, the first [of beings], and I am also the last, and besides Me there is no God," concerning the Father of the universe, do also speak of our Lord Jesus Christ. "A Son," they say, has been given to us, on whose shoulder the government is from above; and His name is called the Angel of great counsel, Wonderful, Counsellor, the strong and mighty God." And concerning His incarnation, "Behold, a virgin shall be with Child, and shall bring forth a Son; and they shall call his name Immanuel." And concerning the passion, "He was led as a sheep to the slaughter; and as a lamb before her shearers is dumb, I also was an innocent lamb led to be sacrificed."

Chapter IV.—Continuation.

The Evangelists, too, when they declared that the one Father was "the only true God," did not omit what concerned our Lord, but wrote: "In the beginning was the Word, and the Word was with God, and the Word was God. The same was in the beginning with God. All things were made by Him, and without Him was not anything made that was made." And concerning the incarnation: "The Word," says [the Scripture], "became flesh, and dwelt among us." And again: "The book of the generation of Jesus Christ, the son of David, the son of Abraham." And those very apostles, who said "that there is one God," said also that "there is one Mediator between God and men." Nor were they ashamed of the incarnation and the passion. For what says [one]? "The man Christ Jesus, who gave Himself" for the life and salvation of the world.

Chapter V.—Denunciation of false teachers.

Whosoever, therefore, declares that there is but one God, only so as to take away the divinity of Christ, is a devil, and an enemy of all righteousness. He also that confesses Christ, yet not as the Son of the Maker of the world, but of some other unknown being, different from Him whom the law and the prophets have proclaimed, this man is an instrument of the devil. And he that rejects the incarnation, and is ashamed of the cross for which I am in bonds, this man is antichrist. Moreover, he who affirms Christ to be a mere man is accursed, according to the [declaration of the] prophet, since he puts not his trust in God, but in man. Wherefore also he is unfruitful, like the wild myrtle-tree.

Chapter VI.—Renewed cautions.

These things I write to you, thou new olive-tree of Christ, not that I am aware you hold any such opinions, but that I may put you on your guard, as a father does his children. Beware, therefore, of those that hasten to work mischief, those "enemies of the cross of Christ, whose end is destruction, whose glory is in their shame." Beware of those "dumb dogs," those trailing serpents, those scaly dragons, those asps, and basilisks, and scorpions. For these are subtle wolves, and apes that mimic the appearance of men.

Chapter VII.—Exhortation to consistency of conduct.

Ye have been the disciples of Paul and Peter; do not lose what was committed to your trust. Keep in remembrance Euodias, your deservedly-blessed pastor, into whose hands the government over you was first entrusted by the apostles. Let us not bring disgrace upon our Father. Let us prove ourselves His true-born children, and not bastards. Ye know after what manner I have acted among you. The things which, when present, I spoke to you, these same, when absent, I now write to you. "If any man love not the Lord Jesus Christ, let him be Anathema." Be ye followers of me. My soul be for yours, when I attain to Jesus. Remember my bonds.

Chapter VIII.—Exhortations to the presbyters and others.

Ye presbyters, "feed the flock which is among you," till God shall show who is to hold the rule over you. For "I am now ready to be offered," that I "may win Christ." Let the deacons know of what dignity they are, and let them study to be blameless, that they may be the followers of Christ. Let the people be subject to the presbyters and the deacons. Let the virgins know to whom they have consecrated themselves.

Chapter IX.—Duties of husbands, wives, parents, and children.

Let the husbands love their wives, remembering

that, at the creation, one woman, and not many, was given to one man. Let the wives honor their husbands, as their own flesh; and let them not presume to address them by their names. Let them also be chaste, reckoning their husbands as their only partners, to whom indeed they have been united according to the will of God. Ye parents, impart a holy training to your children. Ye children, "honor your parents, that it may be well with you."

Chapter X.—Duties of masters and servants.

Ye masters, do not treat your servants with haughtiness, but imitate patient Job, who declares, "I did not despise the cause of my man-servant, or of my maid-servant, when they contended with me. For what in that case shall I do when the Lord makes an inquisition regarding me?" And you know what follows. Ye servants, do not provoke your masters to anger in anything, lest ye become the authors of incurable mischiefs to yourselves.

Chapter XI.—Inculcation of various moral duties.

Let no one addicted to idleness eat, lest he become a wanderer about, and a whoremonger. Let drunkenness, anger, envy, reviling, clamor, and blasphemy "be not so much as named among you." Let not the widows live a life of pleasure, lest they wax wanton against the word. Be subject to Cæsar in everything in which subjection implies no [spiritual] danger. Provoke not those that rule over you to wrath, that you may give no occasion against yourselves to those that seek for it. But as to the practice of magic, or the impure love of boys, or murder, it is superfluous to write to you, since such vices are forbidden to be committed even by the Gentiles. I do not issue commands on these points as if I were an apostle; but, as your fellow-servant, I put you in mind of them.

Chapter XII.—Salutations.

I salute the holy presbytery. I salute the sacred deacons, and that person most dear to me, whom may I behold, through the Holy Spirit, occupying my place when I shall attain to Christ. My soul be in place of his. I salute the sub-deacons, the readers, the singers, the doorkeepers, the laborers, the exorcists, the confessors. I salute the keepers of the holy gates, the deaconesses in Christ. I salute the virgins betrothed to Christ, of whom may I have joy in the Lord Jesus. I salute the people of the Lord, from the smallest to the greatest, and all my sisters in the Lord.

Chapter XIII.—Salutations continued.

I salute Cassian and his partner in life, and their very dear children. Polycarp, that most worthy bishop, who is also deeply interested in you, salutes you; and to him I have commended you in the Lord. The whole Church of the Smyrnæans, indeed, is mindful of you in their prayers in the Lord. Onesimus, the pastor of the Ephesians, salutes you. Damas, the bishop of Magnesia, salutes you. Polybius, bishop of the Trallians, salutes you. Philo and Agathopus, the deacons, my companions, salute you, "Salute one another with a holy kiss."

Chapter XIV.—Conclusion.

I write this letter to you from Philippi. May He who is alone unbegotten, keep you steadfast both in the spirit and in the flesh, through Him who was begotten before time began! And may I behold you in the kingdom of Christ! I salute him who is to bear rule over you in my stead: may I have joy of him in the Lord! Fare ye well in God, and in Christ, being enlightened by the Holy Spirit.

The Epistle of Ignatius to Hero, a Deacon of Antioch

Ignatius, who is also called Theophorus, to Hero, the deacon of Christ, and the servant of God, a man honored by God, and most dearly loved as well as esteemed, who carries Christ and the Spirit within him, and who is mine own son in faith and love: Grace, mercy, and peace from Almighty God, and from Christ Jesus our Lord, His only-begotten Son, "who gave Himself for our sins, that He might deliver us from the present evil world," and preserve us unto His heavenly kingdom.

Chapter I.—Exhortations to earnestness and moderation.

I Exhort thee in God, that thou add [speed] to thy course, and that thou vindicate thy dignity. Have a care to preserve concord with the saints. Bear [the burdens of] the weak, that "thou mayest fulfil the law of Christ." Devote thyself to fasting and prayer, but not beyond measure, lest thou destroy thyself thereby. Do not altogether abstain from wine and flesh, for these things are not to be viewed with abhorrence, since [the Scripture] saith, "Ye shall eat the good things of the earth." And again, "Ye shall eat flesh even as herbs." And again, "Wine makes glad the heart of man, and oil exhilarates, and bread strengthens him." But all are to be used with moderation, as being the gifts of God. "For who shall eat or who shall drink without Him? For if anything be beautiful, it is His; and if anything be good, it is His." Give attention to reading, that thou mayest not only thyself know the laws, but mayest also explain them to others, as the earnest servant of God. "No man that warreth entangles himself with the affairs of this life, that he may please him who hath chosen him to be a soldier; and if a man also strive for masteries, yet is he not crowned except he strive lawfully." I that am in bonds pray that my soul may be in place of yours.

Chapter II.—Cautions against false teachers.

Everyone that teaches anything beyond what is commanded, though he be [deemed] worthy of credit, though he be in the habit of fasting, though he live in continence, though he work miracles, though he have the gift of prophecy, let him be in thy sight as a wolf in sheep's clothing, laboring for the destruction of the sheep. If any one denies the cross, and is ashamed of the passion, let him be to thee as the adversary himself. "Though he gives all his goods to feed the poor, though he remove mountains, though he give his body to be burned," let him be regarded by thee as abominable. If anyone makes light of the law or the prophets, which Christ fulfilled at His coming, let him be to thee as antichrist. If anyone says that the Lord is a mere man, he is a Jew, a murderer of Christ.

Chapter III.—Exhortations as to ecclesiastical duties.

"Honor widows that are widows indeed." Be the friend of orphans; for God is "the Father of the fatherless, and the Judge of the widows." Do nothing without the bishops; for they are priests, and thou a servant of the priests. They baptize, offer sacrifice, ordain, and lay on hands; but thou ministers to them, as the holy Stephen did at Jerusalem to James and the presbyters. Do not neglect the sacred meetings [of the saints]; inquire after every one by name. "Let no man despise thy youth, but be thou an example to the believers, both in word and conduct."

Chapter IV.—Servants and women are not to be despised.

Be not ashamed of servants, for we possess the same nature in common with them. Do not hold women in abomination, for they have given thee birth, and brought thee up. It is fitting, therefore, to love those that were the authors of our birth (but only in the Lord), inasmuch as a man can produce no children without a woman. It is right, therefore, that we should honor those who have had a part in giving us birth. "Neither is the man without the woman, nor the woman without the man," except in the case of those who were first formed. For the body of Adam was made out of the four elements, and that of Eve out of the side of Adam. And, indeed, the altogether peculiar birth of the Lord was of a virgin alone. [This took place] not as if the lawful union [of man and wife] were abominable, but such a kind of birth was fitting to God. For it became the Creator not to make use of the ordinary method of generation, but of one that was singular and strange, as being the Creator.

Chapter V.—Various relative duties.

Flee from haughtiness, "for the Lord resisted the proud." Abhor falsehood, for says [the Scripture], "Thou shalt destroy all them that speak lies." Guard against envy, for its author is the devil, and his successor Cain, who envied his brother, and out of envy committed murder. Exhort my sisters to love God, and be content with their own husbands only. In like manner, exhort my brethren also to be content with their own wives. Watch over the virgins, as the precious treasures of Christ. Be long-suffering, that thou mayest be great in wisdom. Do not neglect the poor, in so far as thou art prosperous. For "by alms and fidelity sins are purged away."

Chapter VI—Exhortations to purity and caution.

Keep thyself pure as the habitation of God. Thou art the temple of Christ. Thou art the instrument of the Spirit. Thou knows in what way I have brought thee up. Though I am the least of men, do thou seek to follow me, be thou an imitator of my conduct. I do not glory in the world, but in the Lord. I exhort Hero, my son; "but let him that glories, glory in the Lord." May I have joy of thee, my dear son, whose guardian may He be who is the only unbegotten God, and the Lord Jesus Christ! Do not believe all persons, do not place confidence in all; nor let any man get the better of thee by flattery. For many are the ministers of Satan; and "he that is hasty to believe is light of heart."

Chapter VII.—Solemn charge to Hero, as future bishop of Antioch.

Keep God in remembrance, and thou shalt never sin. Be not double-minded in thy prayers; for blessed is he who doubted not. For I believe in the Father of the Lord Jesus Christ, and in His only-begotten Son, that God will show me, Hero, upon my throne. Add speed, therefore, to thy course. I charge thee before the God of the universe, and before Christ, and in the presence of the Holy Spirit, and of the ministering ranks [of angels], keep in safety that deposit which I and Christ have committed to thee, and do not judge thyself unworthy of those things which have been shown by God [to me] concerning thee. I hand over to thee the Church of Antioch. I have commended you to Polycarp in the Lord Jesus Christ.

Chapter VIII.—Salutations.

The bishops, Onesimus, Bitus, Damas, Polybius, and all they of Philippi (whence also I have written to thee), salute thee in Christ. Salute the presbytery worthy of God: salute my holy fellow-deacons, of whom may I have joy in Christ, both in the flesh and in the spirit. Salute the people of the Lord, from the smallest to the greatest, everyone by name; whom I commit to thee as Moses did [the Israelites] to Joshua, who was their leader after him. And do not reckon this which I have said presumptuous on my part; for although we are not such as they were, yet we at least pray that we may be so, since indeed we are the children of Abraham. Be strong, therefore, O Hero, like a hero, and like a man. For from henceforth thou shalt lead in and out the people of the Lord that are in Antioch, and so "the congregation of the Lord shall not be as sheep which have no shepherd."

Chapter IX.—Concluding salutations and instructions.

Salute Cassian, my host, and his most serious-minded partner in life, and their very dear children, to whom may "God grant that they find mercy of the Lord in that day," on account of their ministrations to us, whom also I commend to thee in Christ. Salute by name all the faithful in Christ that are at Laodicea. Do not neglect those at Tarsus, but look after them steadily, confirming them in the Gospel. I salute in the Lord, Maris the bishop of Neapolis, near Anazarbus. Salute thou also Mary my daughter, distinguished both for gravity and erudition, as also "the Church which is in her house." May my soul be in place of hers: she is the very pattern of pious women. May the Father of Christ, by His only begotten Son, preserve thee in good health, and of high repute in all things, to a very old age, for the benefit of the Church of God! Farewell in the Lord, and pray thou that I may be perfected.

The Epistle of Ignatius to the Philippians

Ignatius, who is also called Theophorus, to the Church of God which is at Philippi, which has obtained mercy in faith, and patience, and love unfeigned: Mercy and peace from God the Father, and the Lord Jesus Christ, "who is the Savior of all men, specially of them that believe."

Chapter I.—Reason for writing the epistle.

Being mindful of your love and of your zeal in Christ, which ye have manifested towards us, we thought it fitting to write to you, who display such a godly and spiritual love to the brethren, to put you in remembrance of your Christian course, "that ye all speak the same thing, being of one mind, thinking the same thing, and walking by the same rule of faith," as Paul admonished you. For if there is one God of the universe, the Father of Christ, "of whom are all things;" and one Lord Jesus Christ, our [Lord], "by whom are all things;" and also one Holy Spirit, who wrought in Moses, and in the prophets and apostles; and also one baptism, which is administered that we should have fellowship with the death of the Lord; and also one elect Church; there ought likewise to be but one faith in respect to Christ. For "there is one Lord, one faith, one baptism; one God and Father of all, who is through all, and in all."

Chapter II.—Unity of the three divine persons.

There is then one God and Father, and not two or three; One who is; and there is no other besides Him, the only true [God]. For "the Lord thy God," saith [the Scripture], "is one Lord." And again, "Hath not one God created us? Have we not all one Father? And there is also one Son, God the Word. For "the only-begotten Son," saith [the Scripture], "who is in the bosom of the Father." And again, "One Lord Jesus Christ." And in another place, "What is His name, or what His Son's name, that we may know?" And there is also one Paraclete. For "there is also," saith [the Scripture], "one Spirit," since "we have been called in one hope of our calling." And again, "We have drunk of one Spirit," with what follows. And it is manifest that all these gifts [possessed by believers] "worked one and the self-same Spirit." There are not then either three Fathers, or three Sons, or three Paracletes, but one Father, and one Son, and one Paraclete. Wherefore also the Lord, when He sent forth the apostles to make disciples of all nations, commanded them to "baptize in the name of the Father, and of the Son, and of the Holy Ghost," not unto one [person] having three names, nor into three [persons] who became incarnate, but into three possessed of equal honor.

Chapter III.—Christ was truly born, and died.

For there is but One that became incarnate, and that neither the Father nor the Paraclete, but the Son only, [who became so] not in appearance or imagination, but in reality. For "the Word became flesh." For "Wisdom builded for herself a house." And God the Word was born as man, with a body, of the Virgin, without any intercourse of man. For [it is written], "A virgin shall conceive in her womb, and bring forth a son." He was then truly born, truly grew up, truly ate and drank, was truly crucified, and died, and rose again. He who believes these things, as they really were, and as they really took place, is blessed. He who believeth them not is no less accursed than those who crucified the Lord. For the prince of this world rejoices when any one denies the cross, since he knows that the confession of the cross is his own destruction. For that is the trophy which has been raised up against his power, which when he sees, he shudders, and when he hears of, is afraid.

Chapter IV.—The malignity and folly of Satan.

And indeed, before the cross was erected, he (Satan) was eager that it should be so; and he "wrought" [for this end] "in the children of disobedience." He wrought in Judas, in the Pharisees, in the Sadducees, in the old, in the young, and in the priests. But when it was just about to be erected, he was troubled, and infused repentance into the traitor, and pointed him to a rope to hang himself with, and taught him [to die by] strangulation. He terrified also the silly woman, disturbing her by dreams; and he, who had tried every means to have the cross prepared, now endeavored to put a stop to its erection; not that he was influenced by repentance on account of the greatness of his crime (for in that case he would not be utterly depraved), but because he perceived his own destruction [to be at hand]. For the cross of Christ was the beginning of his condemnation, the beginning of his death, the beginning of his destruction. Wherefore, also, he works in some that they should deny the cross, be ashamed of the passion, call the death an appearance, mutilate and explain away the birth of the Virgin, and calumniate the [human] nature itself as being abominable. He fights along with the Jews to a denial of the cross, and with the Gentiles to the calumniating of Mary, who are heretical in holding that Christ possessed a mere phantasmal body. For the leader of all wickedness assumes manifold forms, beguiler of men as he is, inconsistent, and even contradicting himself, projecting one course and then following another. For he is wise to do evil, but as to what good may be he is totally ignorant. And indeed he is full of ignorance, on account of his voluntary want of reason: for how can he be deemed anything else who does not perceive reason when it lies at his very feet?

Chapter V.—Apostrophe to Satan.

For if the Lord were a mere man, possessed of a soul and body only, why dost thou mutilate and explain away His being born with the common nature of humanity? Why dost thou call the passion a mere appearance, as if it were any strange thing happening to a [mere] man? And why dost thou reckon the death of a mortal to be simply an imaginary death? But if, [on the other hand,] He is both God and man, then why dost thou call it unlawful to style Him "the Lord of glory," who is by nature unchangeable? Why dost thou say that it is unlawful to declare of the Lawgiver who possesses a human soul, "The Word was made flesh," and was a perfect man, and not merely one dwelling in a man? But how came this magician into existence, who of old formed all nature that can be apprehended either by the senses or intellect, according to the will of the Father; and, when He became incarnate, healed every kind of disease and infirmity?

Chapter VI.—Continuation.

And how can He be but God, who raises up the dead, sends away the lame sound of limb, cleanses the lepers, restores sight to the blind, and either increases or transmutes existing substances, as the five loaves and the two fishes, and the water which became wine, and who puts to flight thy whole host by a mere word? And why dost thou abuse the nature of the Virgin, and style her members disgraceful, since thou didst of old display such in public processions, and didst order them to be exhibited naked, males in the sight of females, and females to stir up the unbridled lust of males? But now these are reckoned by thee disgraceful, and thou pretends to be full of modesty, thou spirit of fornication, not knowing that then only anything becomes disgraceful when it is polluted by wickedness. But when sin is not present, none of the things that have been created are shameful, none of them evil, but all very good. But inasmuch as thou art blind, thou reviles these things.

Chapter VII.—Continuation: inconsistency of Satan.

And how, again, does Christ not at all appear to thee to be of the Virgin, but to be God over all, and the Almighty? Say, then, who sent Him? Who was Lord over Him? And whose will did He obey? And what laws did He fulfil, since He was subject neither to the will nor power of anyone? And while you deny that Christ was born, you affirm that the unbegotten was begotten, and that He who had no beginning was nailed to the cross, by whose permission I am unable to say. But thy changeable tactics do not escape me, nor am I ignorant that thou art wont to walk with slanting and uncertain steps. And thou art ignorant who really was born, thou who pretends to know everything.

Chapter VIII.—Continuation: ignorance of Satan.

For many things are unknown to thee; [such as the following]: the virginity of Mary; the wonderful birth; Who it was that became incarnate; the star which guided those who were in the east; the Magi who presented gifts; the salutation of the archangel to the Virgin; the marvelous conception of her that was betrothed; the announcement of the boy-forerunner respecting the son of the Virgin, and his leaping in the womb on account of what was foreseen; the songs of the angels over Him that was born; the glad tidings announced to the shepherds; the fear of Herod lest his kingdom should be taken from him; the command to slay the infants; the removal into Egypt, and the return from that country to the same region; the infant swaddling-bands; the human registration; the nourishing by means of milk; the name of father given to Him who did not beget; the manger because there was not room [elsewhere]; no human preparation [for the Child]; the gradual growth, human speech, hunger, thirst, journeyings, weariness; the offering of sacrifices and then also circumcision, baptism; the voice of God over Him that was baptized, as to who He was and whence [He had come]; the testimony of the Spirit and the Father from above; the voice of John the prophet when it signified the passion by the appellation of "the Lamb;" the performance of divers miracles, manifold healings; the rebuke of the Lord ruling both the sea and the winds; evil spirits expelled; thou thyself subjected to torture, and, when afflicted by the power of Him who had been manifested, not having it in thy power to do anything.

Chapter IX.—Continuation: ignorance of Satan.

Seeing these things, thou was in utter perplexity. And thou was ignorant that it was a virgin that should bring forth; but the angels' song of praise struck thee with astonishment, as well as the adoration of the Magi, and the appearance of the star. Thou didst revert to thy state of [willful] ignorance, because all the circumstances seemed to thee trifling; for thou didst deem the swaddling-bands, the circumcision, and the nourishment by means of milk contemptible: these things appeared to thee unworthy of God. Again, thou didst behold a man who remained forty days and nights without tasting human food, along with ministering angels at whose presence thou didst shudder, when first of all thou hadst seen Him baptized as a common man, and knewest not the reason thereof. But after His [lengthened] fast thou didst again assume thy wonted audacity, and didst tempt Him when hungry, as if He had been an ordinary man, not knowing who He was. For thou saidst, "If thou be the Son of God, command that these stones be made bread." Now, this expression, "If thou be the Son," is an indication of ignorance. For if thou hadst possessed real knowledge, thou wouldst have understood that the Creator can with equal ease both create what does not exist, and change that which already has a being. And thou tempted by means of hunger Him who nourished all that require food. And thou tempted the very "Lord of glory," forgetting in thy malevolence that "man shall not live by bread alone, but by every word that proceeded out of the mouth of God." For if thou hadst known that He was the Son of God, thou wouldst also have understood that He who had kept his body from feeling any want for forty days and as many nights, could have also done the same forever. Why, then, does He suffer hunger? In order to prove that He had assumed a body subject to the same feelings as those of ordinary men. By the first fact He showed that He was God, and by the second that He was also man.

Chapter X.—Continuation: audacity of Satan.

Darest thou, then, who didst fall "as lightning" from the very highest glory, to say to the Lord, "Cast thyself down from hence [to Him] to whom the things that are not are reckoned as if they were, and to provoke to a display of vainglory Him that was free from all ostentation? And didst thou pretend to read in Scripture concerning Him: "For He hath given His angels charge concerning Thee, and in their hands they shall bear Thee up, lest thou shouldest dash Thy foot against a stone?" At the same time thou didst pretend to be ignorant of the rest, furtively concealing what [the Scripture] predicted concerning thee and thy servants: "Thou shalt tread upon the adder and the basilisk; the lion and the dragon shall thou trample under foot."

Chapter XI.—Continuation: audacity of Satan.

If, therefore, thou art trodden down under the feet of the Lord, how dost thou tempt Him that cannot be tempted, forgetting that precept of the lawgiver, "Thou shall not tempt the Lord thy God?" Yea, thou even darest, most accursed one, to appropriate the works of God to thyself, and to declare that the dominion over these was delivered to thee. And thou dost set forth thine own fall as an example to the Lord, and dost promise to give Him what is really His own, if He would fall down and worship thee. And how didst thou not shudder, O thou spirit more wicked through thy malevolence than all other wicked spirits, to utter such words against the Lord? Through thine appetite was thou overcome, and through thy vainglory was thou brought to dishonor: through avarice and ambition dost thou [now] draw on [others] to ungodliness. Thou, O Belial, dragon, apostate, crooked serpent, rebel against God, outcast from Christ, alien from the Holy Spirit, exile from the ranks of the angels, reviler of the laws of God, enemy of all that is lawful, who didst rise up against the first-formed of men, and didst drive forth [from obedience to] the commandment [of God] those who had in no respect injured thee; thou who didst raise up against Abel the murderous Cain; thou who didst take arms against Job: dost thou say to the Lord, "If Thou wilt fall down and worship me?" Oh what audacity! Oh what madness! Thou runaway slave, thou incorrigible slave, dost thou rebel against the good Lord? Does thou say to so great a Lord, the God of all that either the mind or the senses can perceive, "If Thou wilt fall down and worship me?"

Chapter XII.—The meek reply of Christ.

But the Lord is long-suffering, and does not reduce to nothing him who in his ignorance dares [to utter] such words, but meekly replies, "Get thee hence, Satan." He does not say, "Get thee behind Me," for it is not possible that he should be converted; but, "Be gone, Satan," to the course which thou hast chosen. "Be gone" to those things to which, through thy malevolence, thou hast been called. For I know Who I am, and by Whom I have been sent, and Whom it behooves Me to worship. For "thou shall worship the Lord thy God, and Him only shalt thou serve." I know the one [God]; I am acquainted with the only [Lord] from whom thou hast become an apostate. I am not an enemy of God; I acknowledge His preeminence; I know the Father, who is the author of my generation.

Chapter XIII.—Various exhortations and directions.

These things, brethren, out of the affection which I entertain for you, I have felt compelled to write, exhorting you with a view to the glory of God, not as if I were a person of any consequence, but simply as a brother. Be ye subject to the bishop, to the presbyters, and to the deacons. Love one another in the Lord, as being the images of God. Take heed, ye husbands, that ye love your wives as your own members. Ye wives also, love your husbands, as being one with them in virtue of your union. If anyone lives in chastity or continence, let him not be lifted up, lest he lose his reward. Do not lightly esteem the festivals. Despise not the period of forty days, for it comprises an imitation of the conduct of the Lord. After the week of the passion, do not neglect to fast on the fourth and sixth days, distributing at the same time of thine abundance to the poor. If anyone fasts on the Lord's Day or on the Sabbath, except on the paschal Sabbath only, he is a murderer of Christ.

Chapter XIV.—Farewells and cautions.

Let your prayers be extended to the Church of

Antioch, whence also I as a prisoner am being led to Rome. I salute the holy bishop Polycarp; I salute the holy bishop Vitalius, and the sacred presbytery, and my fellow-servants the deacons; in whose stead may my soul be found. Once more I bid farewell to the bishop, and to the presbyters in the Lord. If anyone celebrates the Passover along with the Jews, or receives the emblems of their feast, he is a partaker with those that killed the Lord and His apostles.

Chapter XV.—Salutations. Conclusion.

Philo and Agathopus the deacons salute you. I salute the company of virgins, and the order of widows; of whom may I have joy! I salute the people of the Lord, from the least unto the greatest. I have sent you this letter through Euphanius the reader, a man honored of God, and very faithful, happening to meet with him at Rhegium, just as he was going on board ship. Remember my bonds that I may be made perfect in Christ. Fare ye well in the flesh, the soul, and the spirit, while ye think of things perfect, and turn yourselves away from the workers of iniquity, who corrupt the word of truth, and are strengthened inwardly by the grace of our Lord Jesus Christ.

The Epistle of Maria the Proselyte to Ignatius

Mary of Cassobelæ to Ignatius Maria, a proselyte of Jesus Christ, to Ignatius Theophorus, most blessed bishop of the apostolic Church which is at Antioch, beloved in God the Father, and Jesus: Happiness and safety. We all beg for thee joy and health in Him.

Chapter I.—Occasion of the epistle.

Since Christ has, to our wonder, been made known among us to be the Son of the living God, and to have become man in these last times by means of the Virgin Mary, of the seed of David and Abraham, according to the announcements previously made regarding Him and through Him by the company of the prophets, we therefore beseech and entreat that, by thy wisdom, Maris our friend, bishop of our native Neapolis, which is near Zarbus, and Eulogius, and Sobelus the presbyter, be sent to us, that we be not destitute of such as preside over the divine word as Moses also says, "Let the Lord God look out a man who shall guide this people, and the congregation of the Lord shall not be as sheep which have no shepherd."

Chapter II.—Youth may be allied with piety and discretion.

But as to those whom we have named being young men, do not, thou blessed one, have any apprehension. For I would have you know that they are wise about the flesh, and are insensible to its passions, they themselves glowing with all the glory of a hoary head through their own intrinsic merits, and though but recently called as young men to the priesthood. Now, call thou into exercise thy thoughts through the Spirit that God has given to thee by Christ, and thou wilt remember that Samuel, while yet a little child, was called a seer, and was reckoned in the company of the prophets, that he reproved the aged Eli for transgression, since he had honored his infatuated sons above God the author of all things, and had allowed them to go unpunished, when they turned the office of the priesthood into ridicule, and acted violently towards thy people.

Chapter III.—Examples of youthful devotedness.

Moreover, the wise Daniel, while he was a young man, passed judgment on certain vigorous old man, showing them that they were abandoned wretches, and not [worthy to be reckoned] elders, and that, though Jews by extraction, they were Canaanites in practice. And Jeremiah, when on account of his youth he declined the office of a prophet entrusted to him by God, was addressed in these words: "Say not, I am a youth; for thou shalt go to all those to whom I send thee, and thou shalt speak according to all that I command thee; because I am with thee." And the wise Solomon, when only in the twelfth year of his age, had wisdom to decide the important question concerning the children of the two women, when it was unknown to whom these respectively belonged; so that the whole people were astonished at such wisdom in a child, and venerated him as being not a mere youth, but a full-grown man. And he solved the hard questions of the queen of the Ethiopians, which had profit in them as the streams of the Nile [have fertility], in such a manner that that woman, though herself so wise, was beyond measure astonished.

Chapter IV.—The same subject continued.

Josiah also, beloved of God, when as yet he could scarcely speak articulately, convicts those who were possessed of a wicked spirit as being false in their speech, and deceivers of the people. He also reveals the deceit of the demons, and openly exposes those that are no gods; yea, while yet an infant he slays their priests, and overturns their altars, and defiles the place where sacrifices were offered with dead bodies, and throws down the temples, and cuts down the groves, and breaks in pieces the pillars, and breaks open the tombs of the ungodly, that not a relic of the wicked might any longer exist. To such an extent did he display zeal in the cause of godliness, and prove himself a punisher of the ungodly, while he as yet faltered in speech like a child. David, too, who was at once a prophet and a king, and the root of our Savior according to the flesh, while yet a youth is anointed by Samuel to be king. For he himself says in a certain place, "I was small among my brethren, and the youngest in the house of my father."

Chapter V.—Expressions of respect for Ignatius.

But time would fail me if I should endeavor to enumerate all those that pleased God in their youth, having been entrusted by God with either the prophetical, the priestly, or the kingly office. And those which have been mentioned may suffice, by way of bringing the subject to thy remembrance. But I entreat thee not to reckon me presumptuous or ostentatious [in writing as I have done]. For I have set forth these statements, not as instructing thee, but simply as suggesting the matter to the remembrance of my father in God. For I know my own place, and do not compare myself with such as you. I salute thy holy clergy, and thy Christ-loving people who are ruled under thy care as their pastor. All the faithful with us salute thee. Pray, blessed shepherd, that I may be in health as respects God.

The Epistle of Ignatius to Mary at Neapolis, Near Zarbus.

Ignatius, who is also called Theaphorus, to her who has obtained mercy through the grace of the most high God the Father, and Jesus Christ the Lord, who died for us, to Mary, my daughter, most faithful, worthy of God, and bearing Christ [in her heart], wishes abundance of happiness in God.

Chapter I.—Acknowledgment of her excellence and wisdom.

Sight indeed is better than writing, inasmuch as, being one of the company of the senses, it not only, by communicating proofs of friendship, honors him who receives them, but also, by those which it in turn receives, enriches the desire for better things. But the second harbor of refuge, as the phrase runs, is the practice of writing, which we have received, as a convenient haven, by thy faith, from so great a distance, seeing that by means of a letter we have learned the excellence that is in thee. For the souls of the good, O thou wisest of women! Resemble fountains of the purest water; for they allure by their beauty passers-by to drink of them, even though these should not be thirsty. And thy intelligence invites us, as by a word of command, to participate in those divine draughts which gush forth so abundantly in thy soul.

Chapter II.—His own condition.

But I, O thou blessed woman, not being now so much my own master as in the power of others, am driven along by the varying wills of many adversaries, being in one sense in exile, in another in prison, and in a third in bonds. But I pay no regard to these things. Yea, by the injuries inflicted on me through them, I acquire all the more the character of a disciple, that I may attain to Jesus Christ. May I enjoy the torments which are prepared for me, seeing that "the sufferings of this present time are not worthy [to be compared] with the glory which shall be revealed in us."

Chapter III.—He had complied with her request.

I have gladly acted as requested in thy letter, having no doubt respecting those persons whom thou didst prove to be men of worth. For I am sure that thou barest testimony to them in the exercise of a godly judgment, and not through the influence of carnal favor. And thy numerous quotations of Scripture passages exceedingly delighted me, which, when I had read, I had no longer a single doubtful thought respecting the matter. For I did not hold that those things were simply to be glanced over by my eyes, of which I had received from thee such an incontrovertible demonstration. May I be in place of thy soul, because thou loves Jesus, the Son of the living God. Wherefore also He Himself says to thee, "I love them that love Me; and those that seek Me shall find peace."

Chapter IV.—Commendation and exhortation.

Now it occurs to me to mention, that the report is true which I heard of thee whilst thou was at Rome with the blessed father Linus, whom the deservedly-blessed Clement, a hearer of Peter and Paul, has now succeeded. And by this time thou hast added a hundredfold to thy reputation; and may thou, O woman! Still further increase it. I greatly desired to come unto you, that I might have rest with you; but "the way of man is not in himself." For the military guard [under which I am kept] hinders my purpose, and does not permit me to go further. Nor indeed, in the state I am now in, can I either do or suffer anything. Wherefore deeming the practice of writing the second resource of friends for their mutual encouragement, I salute thy sacred soul, beseeching of thee to add still further to thy vigor. For our present labor is but little, while the reward which is expected is great.

Chapter V.—Salutations and good wishes.

Avoid those that deny the passion of Christ, and His birth according to the flesh: and there are many at present who suffer under this disease. But it would be absurd to admonish thee on other points, seeing that thou art perfect in every good work and word, and able also to exhort others in Christ. Salute all that are like-minded with thyself, and who hold fast to their salvation in Christ. The presbyters and deacons, and above all the holy Hero, salute thee. Cassian my host salutes thee, as well as my sister, his wife, and their very dear children. May the Lord sanctify thee for evermore in the enjoyment both of bodily and spiritual health, and may I see thee in Christ obtaining the crown!

The Epistle of Ignatius to St. John the Apostle

Ignatius, and the brethren who are with him, to John the holy presbyter.

We are deeply grieved at thy delay in strengthening us by thy addresses and consolations. If thy absence be prolonged, it will disappoint many of us. Hasten then to come, for we believe that it is expedient. There are also many of our women here, who are desirous to see Mary [the mother] of Jesus, and wish day by day to run off from us to you, that they may meet with her, and touch those breasts of hers which nourished the Lord Jesus, and may inquire of her respecting some rather secret matters. But Salome also, [the daughter of Anna,] whom thou loves, who stayed with her five months at Jerusalem, and some other well-known persons, relate that she is full of all graces and all virtues, after the manner of a virgin, fruitful in virtue and grace. And, as they report, she is cheerful in persecutions and afflictions, free from murmuring in the midst of penury and want, grateful to those that injure her, and rejoices when exposed to troubles: she sympathizes with the wretched and the afflicted as sharing in their afflictions, and is not slow to come to their assistance. Moreover, she shines forth gloriously as contending in the fight of faith against the pernicious conflicts of vicious principles or conduct. She is the lady of our new religion and repentance, and the handmaid among the faithful of all works of piety. She is indeed devoted to the humble, and she humbles herself more devotedly than the devoted, and is wonderfully magnified by all, while at the same time she suffers detraction from the Scribes and Pharisees. Besides these points, many relate to us numerous other things regarding her. We do not, however, go so far as to believe all in every particular; nor do we mention such to thee. But, as we are informed by those who are worthy of credit, there is in Mary the mother of Jesus an angelic purity of nature allied with the nature of humanity. And such reports as these have greatly excited our emotions, and urge us eagerly to desire a sight of this (if it be lawful so to speak) heavenly prodigy and most sacred marvel. But do thou in haste comply with this our desire; and fare thou well. Amen.

A Second Epistle of Ignatius to St. John.

His friend Ignatius to John the holy presbyter.

If thou wilt give me leave, I desire to go up to Jerusalem, and see the faithful saints who are there, especially Mary the mother, whom they report to be an object of admiration and of affection to all. For who would not rejoice to behold and to address her who bore the true God from her own womb, provided he is a friend of our faith and religion? And in like manner [I desire to see] the venerable James, who is surnamed Just, whom they relate to be very like Christ Jesus in appearance, in life, and in method of conduct, as if he were a twin-brother of the same womb. They say that, if I see him, I see also Jesus Himself, as to all the features and aspect of His body. Moreover, [I desire to see] the other saints, both male and female. Alas! Why do I delay? Why am I kept back? Kind teacher, bid me hasten [to fulfil my wish], and fare thou well. Amen.

The Epistle of Ignatius to the Virgin Mary

Her friend Ignatius to the Christ-bearing Mary.

Thou oughtest to have comforted and consoled me who am a neophyte, and a disciple of thy [beloved] John. For I have heard things wonderful to tell respecting thy [son] Jesus, and I am astonished by such a report. But I desire with my whole heart to obtain information concerning the things which I have heard from thee, who was always intimate and allied with Him, and who was acquainted with [all] His secrets. I have also written to thee at another time, and have asked thee concerning the same things. Fare thou well; and let the neophytes who are with me be comforted of thee, and by thee, and in thee. Amen.

Reply of the Blessed Virgin to this Letter.

The lowly handmaid of Christ Jesus to Ignatius, her beloved fellow-disciple.

The things which thou hast heard and learned from John concerning Jesus are true. Believe them, cling to them, and hold fast the profession of that Christianity which thou hast embraced, and conform thy habits and life to thy profession. Now I will come in company with John to visit thee, and those that are with thee. Stand fast in the faith, and show thyself a man; nor let the fierceness of persecution move thee, but let thy spirit be strong and rejoice in God thy Savior. Amen.

Introductory Note to the Martyrdom of Ignatius

The learned dissertation of Pearson, on the difficulties of reconciling the supposed year of the martyrdom with the history of Trajan, etc., is given entire in Jacobson (vol. ii. p. 524), against the decision of Usher for a.d.107. Pearson accepts a.d.116. Consult also the preface of Dr. Thomas Smith, in the same work (p. 518), on the text of the original and of the Latin versions, and on the credibility of the narrative. Our learned translators seem to think the text they have used, to be without interpolation. If the simple-minded faithful of those days, so near the age of miracles, appear to us, in some degree, enthusiasts, let us remember the vision of Col. Gardiner, accredited by Doddridge, Lord Lyttleton's vision (see Boswell, anno 1784, chap. xi.), accepted by Johnson and his contemporaries, and the interesting narrative of the pious Mr. Tennent of New Jersey, attested by so many excellent and intelligent persons, almost of our own times.

The following is the Introductory Notice of the translators:—

The following account of the martyrdom of Ignatius professes, in several passages, to have been written by those who accompanied him on his voyage to Rome, and were present on the occasion of his death (chaps. v. vi. vii.). And if the genuineness of this narrative, as well as of the Ignatian Epistles, be admitted, there can be little doubt that the persons in question were Philo and Agathopus, with Crocus perhaps, all of whom are mentioned by Ignatius (Epist. to Smyr., chap. x.; to Philad., chap. xi.; to Rom., chap. x.) as having attended him on that journey to Rome which resulted in his martyrdom. But doubts have been started, by Daillé and others, as to the date and authorship of this account. Some of these rest upon internal considerations, but the weightiest objection is found in the fact that no reference to this narrative is to be traced during the first six centuries of our era. This is certainly a very suspicious circumstance, and may well give rise to some hesitation in ascribing the authorship to the immediate companions and friends of Ignatius. On the other hand, however, this account of the death of Ignatius is in perfect harmony with the particulars recounted by Eusebius and Chrysostom regarding him. Its comparative simplicity, too, is greatly in its favor. It makes no reference to the legends which by and by connected themselves with the name of Ignatius. As is well known, he came in course of time to be identified with the child whom Christ (Matt. xviii. 2) set before His disciples as a pattern of humility. It was said that the Savior took him up in His arms, and that hence Ignatius derived his name of Theophorus; that is, according to the explanation which this legend gives of the word, one carried by God. But in chap. ii. of the following narrative we find the term explained to mean, "One who has Christ in his breast;" and this simple explanation, with the entire silence preserved as to the marvels afterwards connected with the name of Ignatius, is certainly a strong argument in favor of the early date and probable genuineness of the account. Some critics, such as Usher and Grabe, have reckoned the latter part of the narrative spurious, while accepting the former; but there appears to be a unity about it which requires us either to accept it in toto, or to reject it altogether.

The Martyrdom of Ignatius

Chapter I.—Desire of Ignatius for martyrdom.

When Trajan, not long since, succeeded to the empire of the Romans, Ignatius, the disciple of John the apostle, a man in all respects of an apostolic character, governed the Church of the Antiochians with great care, having with difficulty escaped the former storms of the many persecutions under Domitian, inasmuch as, like a good pilot, by the helm of prayer and fasting, by the earnestness of his teaching, and by his [constant] spiritual labor, he resisted the flood that rolled against him, fearing [only] lest he should lose any of those who were deficient in courage, or apt to suffer from their simplicity. Wherefore he rejoiced over the tranquil state of the Church, when the persecution ceased for a little time, but was grieved as to himself, that he had not yet attained to a true love to Christ, nor reached the perfect rank of a disciple. For he inwardly reflected, that the confession which is made by martyrdom, would bring him into a yet more intimate relation to the Lord. Wherefore, continuing a few years longer with the Church, and, like a divine lamp, enlightening every one's understanding by his expositions of the [Holy] Scriptures, he [at length] attained the object of his desire.

Chapter II.—Ignatius is condemned by Trajan.

For Trajan, in the ninth year of his reign, being lifted up [with pride], after the victory he had gained over the Scythians and Dacians, and many other nations, and thinking that the religious body of the Christians were yet wanting to complete the subjugation of all things to himself, and [thereupon] threatening them with persecution unless they should agree to worship dæmons, as did all other nations, thus compelled all who were living godly lives either to sacrifice [to idols] or die. Wherefore the noble soldier of Christ [Ignatius], being in fear for the Church of the Antiochians, was, in accordance with his own desire, brought before Trajan, who was at that time staying at Antioch, but was in haste [to set forth] against Armenia and the Parthians. And when he was set before the emperor Trajan, [that prince] said unto him, "Who art thou, wicked wretch, who settest thyself to transgress our commands, and persuades others to do the same, so that they should miserably perish?" Ignatius replied, "No one ought to call Theophorus wicked; for all evil spirits have departed from the servants of God. But if, because I am an enemy to these [spirits], you call me wicked in respect to them, I quite agree with you; for inasmuch as I have Christ the King of heaven [within me], I destroy all the devices of these [evil spirits]." Trajan answered, "And who is Theophorus?" Ignatius replied, "He who has Christ within his breast." Trajan said, "Do we not then seem to you to have the gods in our mind, whose assistance we enjoy in fighting against our enemies?" Ignatius answered, "Thou art in error when thou calls the dæmons of the nations gods. For there is but one God, who made heaven, and earth, and the sea, and all that are in them; and one Jesus Christ, the only-begotten Son of God, whose kingdom may I enjoy." Trajan said, "Do you mean Him who was crucified under Pontius Pilate?" Ignatius replied, "I mean Him who crucified my sin, with him who was the inventor of it, and who has condemned [and cast down] all the deceit and malice of the devil under the feet of those who carry Him in their heart." Trajan said, "Dost thou then carry within thee Him that was crucified?" Ignatius replied, "Truly so; for it is written, 'I will dwell in them, and walk in them.' " Then Trajan pronounced sentence as follows: "We command that Ignatius, who affirms that he carries about within him Him that was crucified, be bound by soldiers, and carried to the great [city] Rome, there to be devoured by the beasts, for the gratification of the people." When the holy martyr heard this sentence, he cried out with joy, "I thank thee, O Lord, that Thou hast vouchsafed to honor me with a perfect love towards Thee, and hast made me to be bound with iron chains, like Thy Apostle Paul." Having spoken thus, he then, with delight, clasped the chains about him; and when he had first prayed for the Church, and commended it with tears to the Lord, he was hurried away by the savage cruelty of the soldiers, like a distinguished ram the leader of a goodly flock, that he might be carried to Rome, there to furnish food to the bloodthirsty beasts.

Chapter III.—Ignatius sails to Smyrna.

Wherefore, with great alacrity and joy, through his desire to suffer, he came down from Antioch to Seleucia, from which place he set sail. And after a great deal of suffering he came to Smyrna, where he disembarked with great joy, and hastened to see the holy Polycarp, [formerly] his fellow-disciple, and [now] bishop of Smyrna. For they had both, in old times, been disciples of St. John the Apostle. Being then brought to him, and having communicated to him some spiritual gifts, and glorying in his bonds, he entreated of him to labor along with him for the fulfilment of his desire; earnestly indeed asking this of the whole Church (for the cities and Churches of Asia had welcomed the holy man through their bishops, and presbyters, and deacons, all hastening to meet him, if by any means they might receive from him some spiritual gift), but above all, the holy Polycarp, that, by means of the wild beasts, he soon disappearing from this world, might be manifested before the face of Christ.

Chapter IV.—Ignatius writes to the churches.

And these things he thus spoke, and thus testified, extending his love to Christ so far as one who was about to secure heaven through his good confession, and the earnestness of those who joined their prayers to his in regard to his [approaching] conflict; and to give a recompense to the Churches, who came to meet him through their rulers, sending letters of thanksgiving to them, which dropped spiritual grace, along with prayer and exhortation. Wherefore, seeing all men so kindly affected towards him, and fearing lest the love of the brotherhood should hinder his zeal towards the Lord, while a fair door of suffering martyrdom was opened to him, he wrote to the Church of the Romans the Epistle which is here subjoined.

(See the Epistle as formerly given.)

Chapter V.—Ignatius is brought to Rome.

Having therefore, by means of this Epistle, settled, as he wished, those of the brethren at Rome who were unwilling [for his martyrdom]; and setting sail from Smyrna (for Christophorus was pressed by the soldiers to hasten to the public spectacles in the mighty [city] Rome, that, being given up to the wild beasts in the sight of the Roman people, he might attain to the crown for which he strove), he [next] landed at Troas. Then, going on from that place to Neapolis, he went [on foot] by Philippi through Macedonia, and on to that part of Epirus which is near Epidamnus; and finding a ship in one of the seaports, he sailed over the Adriatic Sea, and entering from it on the Tyrrhene, he passed by the various islands and cities, until, when Puteoli came in sight, he was eager there to disembark, having a desire to tread in the footsteps of the Apostle Paul. But a violent wind arising did not suffer him to do so, the ship being driven rapidly forwards; and, simply expressing his delight over the love of the brethren in that place, he sailed by. Wherefore, continuing to enjoy fair winds, we were reluctantly hurried on in one day and a night, mourning [as we did] over the coming departure from us of this righteous man. But to him this happened just as he wished, since he was in haste as soon as possible to leave this world, that he might attain to the Lord whom he loved. Sailing then into the Roman harbor, and the unhallowed sports being just about to close, the soldiers began to be annoyed at our slowness, but the bishop rejoicingly yielded to their urgency.

Chapter VI.—Ignatius is devoured by the beasts at Rome.

They pushed forth therefore from the place which is called Portus; and (the fame of all relating to the holy martyr being already spread abroad) we met the brethren full of fear and joy; rejoicing indeed because they were thought worthy to meet with Theophorus, but struck with fear because so eminent a man was being led to death. Now he enjoined some to keep silence who, in their fervent zeal, were saying that they would appease the people, so that they should not demand the destruction of this just one. He being immediately aware of this through the Spirit, and having saluted them all, and begged of them to show a true affection towards him, and having dwelt [on this point] at greater length than in his Epistle, and having persuaded them not to envy him hastening to the Lord, he then, after he had, with all the brethren kneeling [beside him], entreated the Son of God in behalf of the Churches, that a stop might be put to the persecution, and that mutual love might continue among the brethren, was led with all haste into the amphitheater. Then, being immediately thrown in, according to the command of Cæsar given some time ago, the public spectacles being just about to close (for it was then a solemn day, as they deemed it, being that which is called the thirteenth in the Roman tongue, on which the people were wont to assemble in more than ordinary numbers), he was thus cast to the wild beasts close beside the temple, that so by them the desire of the holy martyr Ignatius should be fulfilled, according to that which is written, "The desire of the righteous is acceptable [to God]," to the effect that he might not be troublesome to any of the brethren by the gathering of his remains, even as he had in his Epistle expressed a wish beforehand that so his end might be. For only the harder portions of his holy remains were left, which were conveyed to Antioch and wrapped in linen, as an inestimable treasure left to the holy Church by the grace which was in the martyr.

Chapter VII.—Ignatius appears in a vision after his death.

Now these things took place on the thirteenth day before the Kalends of January, that is, on the twentieth of December, Sura and Senecio being then the consuls of the Romans for the second time. Having ourselves been eye-witnesses of these things, and having spent the whole night in tears within the house, and having entreated the Lord, with bended knees and much prayer, that He would give us weak men full assurance respecting the things which were done, it came to pass, on our falling into a brief slumber, that some of us saw the blessed Ignatius suddenly standing by us and embracing us, while others beheld him again praying for us, and others still saw him dropping with sweat, as if he had just come from his great labor, and standing by the Lord. When, therefore, we had with great joy witnessed these things, and had compared our several visions together, we sang praise to God, the giver of all good things, and expressed our sense of the happiness of the holy [martyr]; and now we have made known to you both the day and the time [when these things happened], that, assembling ourselves together according to the time of his martyrdom, we may have fellowship with the champion and noble martyr of Christ, who trod underfoot the devil, and perfected the course which, out of love to Christ, he had desired, in Christ Jesus our Lord; by whom, and with whom, be glory and power to the Father, with the Holy Spirit, for evermore! Amen.

www.ingramcontent.com/pod-product-compliance
Lightning Source LLC
Chambersburg PA
CBHW060606080526
44585CB00013B/710